PENGUIN BOOKS

An Angel Bit the Bride

James McClelland was born in Melbourne in 1915 and studied at Melbourne and Sydney Universities. As both participant and spectator of one of the most interesting periods in Australia's history, he survived a brief political career as a minister in the Whitlam government to become the first chief judge of the Land and Environment Court of NSW in 1980, and in 1984, commissioner for the Royal Commission into British Nuclear Tests at Maralinga.

He describes himself as 'a child of the Great Depression and a fugitive from religion and Marxism . . . a former lawyer who is clear-sighted about the lawyers; a former judge who is clear-sighted about the judiciary and a present journalist who is clear-sighted about the media'.

He now writes for the *Sydney Morning Herald* and lives in the Blue Mountains with his third wife, Gillian Appleton.

JOHN JENNINGS
STUDIO 22
CULGOA CRESCENT
PAMBULA BEACH N.S.W.

ALSO BY JAMES McCLELLAND:

Stirring the Possum

An ANGEL BIT THE BRIDE and other musings . . .

James McClelland

PENGUIN BOOKS

Penguin Books Australia Ltd
487 Maroondah Highway, PO Box 257
Ringwood, Victoria, 3134, Australia
Penguin Books Ltd
Harmondsworth, Middlesex, England
Viking Penguin Inc.
40 West 23rd Street, New York, NY 10010, USA
Penguin Books Canada Limited
2801 John Street, Markham, Ontario, Canada, L3R 1B4
Penguin Books (N.Z.) Ltd
182-190 Wairau Road, Auckland 10, New Zealand
First published by Penguin Books Australia, 1989
10 9 8 7 6 5 4 3 2 1
Copyright © James McClelland, 1989
All Rights Reserved. Without limiting the rights under copyright
reserved above, no part of this publication may be reproduced,
stored in or introduced into a retrieval system, or transmitted,
in any form or by any means (electronic, mechanical, photocopying,
recording or otherwise), without the prior written permission
of both the copyright owner and the above publisher of this book.
Typeset in Berkeley Old Style by Midland Typesetters, Maryborough
Made and printed in Australia by The Book Printer

CIP

McClelland, J. R. (James Robert), 1915-
   An angel bit the bride and other musings—.
   ISBN 0 14 012831 X.
   I. Title. II. Title : Sydney morning herald.
A828.308

NOTE
The author and publishers gratefully acknowledge the help of the *Sydney Morning
Herald*, the paper in which these articles first appeared. The date of first publication
is included at the end of each article.

CONTENTS

FOREWORD

My first preference for a way to earn a living was to be a journalist. The very word had a slightly bohemian resonance which appealed to my adolescent imagination and, of course, I was always addicted to language. But I came on the labour market in the depths of the Great Depression, I had no connections with the newspaper world and there were no openings to become a cadet.

My career has not been a planned one. I don't suggest I have been a drifter but circumstance has played a larger role than choice in what I have done with my life – or perhaps I should say what life has done with me. That probably applies to most people.

Over the more than fifty years during which I got up every morning to go to work, I observed a gradual change in social attitudes towards the appropriate age for people to retire from the workforce. The idea gradually took hold that not everybody becomes unemployable on the tick of sixty or sixty-five years. My tenure of office as a judge came to an end when I reached the statutory retiring age of seventy in June 1985. My working life was prolonged for another six months by the task of taking part in the preparation and presentation to the Governor-General of the report of the findings of the Royal Commission into the Maralinga nuclear tests, of which I was president.

Then I was put out to pasture. It was a moment I had always feared. I had plenty of interests, but having taken part in some stirring events on the public stage, I did not fancy being relegated to the irrelevance of retirement. I did not relish the idea of being out of it all. I do not play bowls (though I confess to that other allegedly geriatric hobby, pottering in the garden).

I didn't have to grapple for long with this late-life crisis. Early in 1986 I was approached by Eric Beecher, then editor of the *Sydney Morning Herald*, who asked if I would care to write for his paper. I agreed, stipulating that I was to write when I liked about anything I chose. I further insisted that I did not want to be tied to a deadline by having to present my copy for any particular day of the week.

At first I wrote sporadically, contributing perhaps two columns a month. But gradually I became an addict and for the past couple of years my column has – apart from a couple of brief interruptions caused by holidays or pressures of space for more momentous items – appeared once a week.

What I did not bargain for when I picked up my pen was the correspondence which the column provoked. One of the pieces in this collection (*Person from Wallabadah*) deals with this aspect of my new trade.

The pro-royalist, 'Britain-is-still-our-motherland' philosophy has a diminishing appeal in Australia but its diehards can be quite vituperative to those, like me, who regard that view of life as Neanderthal. One such whose sensibilities I had affronted sent me a letter which concluded: 'Underneath your superficial elegance, you are clearly just another bog-Irish lout.'

My openly proclaimed atheism also causes a fair bit of hackle-raising. It has provoked reactions ranging from total disbelief that anybody can question the existence or need for a god, to pity for my benighted condition and earnest attempts to rope me back into the godly flock. The latter are often accompanied by fundamentalist tracts or bible texts, and even – on occasion – exhortatory cassette tapes and prayerbooks.

And there are the antagonists like the person from Wallabadah, who sought to put me in my place by fastening on the inevitable typos which creep into any copy which is (like mine) phoned in to copy takers, as evidence of my basic illiteracy.

From the beginning I took the view that anybody who was sufficiently interested in anything that I wrote – whether the reaction was adverse, favourable or merely curious – to write a letter to me about it deserved a reply. Thus, apart from the odd yobbo or sickening racist, everybody who has written to me has had a reply.

Although this has sometimes involved a certain tedium, I have enjoyed and believe I have profited from this interchange. I have been touched by the many thoughtful, concerned and compassionate people who have taken the time to write, sometimes at considerable length. Of course, it is always gratifying to find that people agree with you; but these letters are particularly welcome – and indeed comforting – in a period in this country when, as I believe, self-interest and greed are too often the norm.

Finally, I must acknowledge the contribution to my development as a columnist of my editors at the *Herald*, Chris Henning and his successor, Scott Milson. Their critical comments and the ideas they suggested have invariably proved useful. My wife Gil is also a stern editor as well as a reliable source of topics when my own brain is blank – the columnist's curse.

So here are some of my less ephemeral jottings for those who may have missed them and those who may be interested to read them again.

James McClelland

AN ANGEL BIT THE BRIDE

My wife (who for reasons lost in the mists of time is jocularly known around here as The Bride) was attacked last week by a dog. Ironically, this attack on a woman who has only recently survived the perils of New York (where, one is led to believe, a mugging occurs every two or three seconds) took place in the sylvan fastnesses of our mountain retreat.

At the time of the attack, The Bride was taking her daily exercise of an hour's cycling. The first I heard that anything was amiss was a call: 'Blue Mountains Hospital here.' As the blood began to freeze in my veins, a pleasant voice assured me that the injury was minor and The Bride's return imminent.

The estimate proved optimistic. It was more than two hours before she appeared, bikeless, pale, heavily bandaged and on crutches. She had been conveyed by the even whiter-faced owners of the cranky dog, who feared no doubt demands for its immediate destruction, or worse, a massive damages suit.

The story unfolds of a family out strolling with its cherished pet ('she's so lovely at home'), throwing sticks for it to retrieve, when into this idyllic scene pedals The Bride. The dog, named Angel with stunning inappropriateness, in an overexcited state induced by its release from the confines of its yard – the only place where it is not devilish – streaks from the bush and fastens a vice-like grip on The Bride's right foot.

The dog's owner succeeds in unlocking its jaws and The Bride dismounts with a mangled ankle, crushed tendons and excruciating pain at any attempt to walk. Several stitches, tetanus and diphtheria injections and x-rays later, she is returned to me for at least a week of enforced immobility.

During the next few days, The Bride is unable to perform the services which many of us husbands, to our shame, take for granted. I am called upon to step into her domestic shoes, and, fresh from my training period during her New York sortie, perform with passable efficiency.

The story gets around among our friends. After condolences are expressed and the probability of The Bride's survival established, the question comes naturally to their lips: 'Of course, you'll sue?'

At this point, I comprehend that the stunned mullet expression on the faces of Angel's owners was not one of unalloyed compassion. They had admitted to The Bride that Angel had previously bitten the person who delivers the milk. The dog had what is known to the police and the crim fraternity as 'form', and they were on notice that it should be restrained.

No doubt, their ashen pallor would have been even more pronounced had they known that the spouse to whom they were delivering Angel's victim had been a personal injury lawyer in an earlier incarnation, or as the larrikins of the law would put it, a 'nello rorter'. (The word 'nello' is a pure expression of ocker verbal creativity. The first thing to be established in an action for personal injury is negligence on the part of the person or persons sued. Negligence was always a difficult word for the Australian tongue to wrap itself around, so it became 'nelligence' and hence 'nello'.)

To help pass the time and revive The Bride's spirits, I recited to her in the style of an old-fashioned nello-rorter (the greatest known exponent of the art is the American trial lawyer Melvin Belli), my opening address to the jury in her claim for $1 575 000.43 damages against Angel's owners, Angel herself and, for more abundant precaution in case The Bride lost her leg, the Blue Mountains Hospital.

Ladies and gentlemen of the jury, my client set out one day with a blown kiss to her aging but doting husband, on her daily bicycle ride through the glades of their beloved Blue Mountains. Little did they know that she would return cruelly maimed, her normally happy disposition soured by a nasty and preventable blow of fate.

Her sufferings will be related to you by the plaintiff herself, by seventeen independent physicians of the highest qualifications, by eleven eminent psychiatrists who will testify to the transformation of a sunny personality into a tetchy nagger, and finally by an honest milkman who will tell you of his daily terror as he attempted to avoid the snarling fangs of this animal, which had obviously had its natural savagery fostered and aggravated by owners with an excessively protective attitude to their possessions.

As we warmed to this game, The Bride and I came up with all sorts of em-Bellishments (pun intended) to this tale of her woes. The jury wept.

It became obvious that we had set our sights too low and I sought leave to amend the writ to a claim of $5 million. Without even retiring, the jury awarded the amount claimed, adding a rider that Angel should be translated to the place where angels belong.

In the past year, a large and lucrative section of the legal work in NSW has disappeared as a result of the Unsworth Government's amendments to the law of negligence in the fields of industrial and motor vehicle accidents.

When I practised in this field, I always wondered how long the bonanza could last. Perhaps the Government has been too Draconian in its changes, but the law as it formerly stood invited exploitation by histrionically gifted legal mediocrities, the paradigm of whom was the late Clive Evatt Senior.

A recent issue of the *Spectator* records these remarks about recent trends in the American tort system: 'Almost any misfortune can be blamed on somebody else. Electrocute yourself breaking into a house? Sue the owner. Crash your car while drunk? Sue the bartender.'

Society should accept responsibility to care for the victims of the blows of fate which modern life inevitably inflicts on an increasingly large number of unfortunate human beings. But surely there is a cost-efficient way of achieving this without making it a playground for lawyers.

We have no intention of suing Angel's owners. I content myself with the hope that they will have been sufficiently frightened by what happened to keep the dog firmly on a leash when they take it out of its yard.

I no longer have much time for the Belli-cose (sorry about that) practice of suing at the drop of a hat (or in the case of some politicians, at the hint of a slur).

Incidentally, The Bride has made a complete recovery.

26 January 1988

PERSON FROM WALLABADAH IS OUT TO GET ME

The mail I receive from readers of this column can be divided into three broad categories: the adulatory, the abusive and the more-in-sorrow-than-in-anger.

I will skip the first, though I will not pretend that it does not please me.

The second is the most entertaining. What appears to rouse more people to put pen to paper than anything else I write is any hint of Anglophobia. The slightest suggestion that the Royals are less than godlike, that Margaret Thatcher has ever had an equal in politics or that Britannia does not still rule the waves is sufficient to bring on an apoplectic riposte from some unreconstructed Anglophile.

One wounded worshipper of the Crown concluded with the remark: 'Despite your superficial elegance, you are obviously just another bog-Irish lout.' If she is still reading my light-hearted effusions, she will have been confirmed in this opinion by my recent tribute to the beauties of Ireland.

But my favourite is a person (gender indeterminate from signature but I will assume male) who evidently picks up the *Herald* every morning, magnifying glass in hand, and scrutinises every word in search of a syntactical error or a mis-spelling or a *mot injuste* (sic).

There are rich pickings in such a trivial pursuit. If, like me, you are a product of the pre-computer, pre-fax era, obliged to dictate your copy over the telephone, and if you are rash enough to use some words that are not common currency, you run the risk that what appears on the printed page will not always be exactly what you wrote.

So, by catching up with modern technology I may soon deprive my occasional correspondent, who hails from Walla-badah, NSW, of his hobby, which may be described as cutting smart-arse McClelland down to size.

A recent display of his superior erudition goes like this:

Congratulations! I knew you could do it. I mean get a foreign expression or quotation right. Hitherto, your attempts have been way off, and though your boobs of course have gone quite unnoticed by the Herald's *semi-literate readership, your struggles have been a cause of concern to your admirers, some of whom are literate.*

I am referring, of course, to your use of the expression faute de mieux *in your timely* Herald *article the other day (about the evils of compulsory voting). When I say you got it right, I should say "almost right". You wrote "faut de . . . ." Still, that's near enough. We all knew, for once, what you meant.*

Frankly, however, I shall be a little sorry personally if – perhaps by taking evening classes – you have mastered the art of foreign allusion. Your howlers in the past have not only enhanced the public stock of harmless gaiety, but sometimes have presented intriguing puzzles.

He went on to instance my use of the term *tant pis*, which came out as *tant tis*. The only count in his indictment to which I plead guilty is a slip of the tongue in an interview with John Pilger in which I referred to Bob Menzies as an 'Anglophobe'. When I saw the program I winced with shame but I'm delighted to know that this further illustration of my verbal fallibility gave rise to some joy in Wallabadah.

Pilger no doubt allowed ABC viewers the credit for enough intelligence to recognise the gaffe for what it was, having a higher regard for them than my correspondent has for his fellow readers of the *Herald*. Until recently I'd not answered him, but when another malapropism in the form of the word 'gambit' crept in instead of 'gamut', I wrote immediately in case he had been having an off day and missed this latest howler.

Turning from the ridiculous to the sublime, I am always touched by the letters from religious people who are sorry for me for missing out on the comforts they find in their belief. The letters are often accompanied by bibles or books of religious instruction, of which I am building quite a collection. The prevailing tone is incredulity that a person holding strong moral beliefs can do so without God. I invariably give them a soft answer as I do not wish to kick away anybody's props. But please, no more literature.

Another category is the cry for help. I get letters from jail inmates claiming (probably quite truthfully in some cases, in the light of what we have recently heard from Queensland) to have been verballed; and requests from greenies to publicise some outrage threatening an environmental treasure. Sometimes I feel like an honorary ombudsman.

Correction of mistaken beliefs also gets a guernsey. The piece on Ireland I referred to above elicited a charming letter from the Irish trade representative in Australia. I had concluded my piece with the words: 'We left Ireland wondering whether backwardness is the price to be paid for the preservation of loveliness.'

My Irish correspondent, while expressing thanks for my praise of the Irish landscape, entered a mild protest, pointing out that Ireland is in fact a country with a healthy export surplus, an inflation rate of 1.8 per cent, very low interest rates, a burgeoning high-tech sector and a young, well-educated population. He went on:

'No lame-duck, decaying, smoke-stack cities. Instead we have had the rapid development of clean, cerebral-intensive information technology industries, or as IBM put it in a recent ad in the *Irish Times* – "Ireland, the land of saints and scholars, systems engineers and software writers".'

If I had not got this letter I may have written, as I was tempted to, after a recent visit to Tasmania: 'Tasmania is Australia's Ireland: small, beautiful and backward.'

The Irish letter saved me from any such dangerous generalisation.

16 December 1988

THE DEMISE OF LADIES AND GENTS

Ladies and gentlemen, you've had your day. The future belongs to men and women.

This thought was provoked by an experience on one of our recent trips to our mountain retreat.

To while away the time and to find out what was on our fellow citizens' minds, we tuned in to Margaret Throsby's talkback program on ABC radio.

One caller, a woman, began by saying: 'I am afraid that the question I had in mind has already been asked by the lady who just spoke to you.'

As we listened we found that most of the female callers referred to other women as 'ladies'.

This propelled us into a short discussion on the status of the term 'lady' in daily currency. In the context in which it had just been used we both found it a little grating. Wouldn't 'woman' have been preferable?

If it has not quite fallen into total disrepute, 'lady' is certainly on the skids. To a modern ear it sounds either classist or sexist, or, worst of all, genteel.

I have no doubt that some excellently educated and progressive-minded young women emerge from institutions like the Presbyterian Ladies' Colleges, without which an Australian city would be incomplete.

But I suspect that the brightest of them might be a little bit fazed if called upon to enunciate the school name in full. It has a mid-Victorian resonance, suggesting that the knowledge of science or literature picked up within its portals ranks a long way down the line after good manners, a proper regard for the school's status and the consciousness of being a cut above the hoi polloi.

At a more basic level, the semantic contest is illustrated by the dilemma over the name of public toilets. Should it remain Gentleman and Ladies, or become just Men and Women?

After all, there is nothing either ladylike or gentlemanly about the elemental human functions to which they cater. Surely there is an argument here for the value-neutral terms which assert no more than that the world is divided into males and females, who prefer to perform those functions separately.

One way around the problem, increasingly prevalent in multilingual societies (like ours) or places (such as airports), is to use symbols instead of words. But this can be confusing.

What would a kilted Scotsman consider to be the appropriate relief station for him? In general, symbols could be more clear-cut than they are in denoting gender difference.

Recently, as I was about to enter a revolving door, a gentleman (obviously) of the old school stepped aside and, with elaborate courtesy, said to a young woman behind him: 'Ladies first.'

Obviously insulted, she glared at him and refused to enter the door before him. His air of wounded bewilderment as he obeyed was that of a member of a species that does not know it is on the way out.

I had already picked up the new protocol of courtesy when a young woman offered me her seat on a bus. She was deferring to age, not sex.

I'm sure the gent of the incident at the door did not mean to be patronising. But that's how the modern young woman saw it.

When the gentlemen used to retire after dinner to enjoy their port and cigars without the presence of their womenfolk (does this still happen anywhere on Earth?), one of them would suggest, so legend has it, at the end of this ritual: 'Well, shall

8

we join the ladies?' It is associations like this that have brought the word into disrepute.

To feminists, of course, it has long been a dirty word, redolent of a mixture of snobbery and male chauvinism. And yet, a lesbian of my acquaintance always refers to her current lover as 'my lady', and I find it hard to detect anything but affection in a male's reference to his wife as 'my old lady'.

So a caution may be in order here. There may be occasions when use of the word may still be considered relatively harmless.

The fate of words is frequently a matter of fashion rather than principle. It is surely pedantic to anathematise a word entirely.

Fashions die hard and adherence to a semantic use which is going or has gone out of fashion (in the case of Margaret Throsby's 'ladies') can sometimes be regarded as no more serious than continuing to adhere to a short-back-and-sides haircut when they are out with all but the punks.

I heard a learned and entertaining scientist, speaking recently on Robyn Williams's Science Show, use the term 'lady gorillas'. For all his mastery of his own discipline he had not caught up with the tendency to express gender differences in plainer terms.

Language is in a state of constant transition. Not everybody is equally attuned to the nuances of linguistic change. To be too censorious about words may sometimes be akin to putting too much stress on the height of the hemline.

This is not to gainsay the seriousness of changes in the use of language. Those changes which are more than just passing fashions usually mirror real changes in social attitudes and behaviour.

The declining status of the word 'lady' is a reflection of the changes in attitudes as between men and women and of a progression away from a hierarchical layering of society in which most females were women, but the more privileged of them were ladies – and many of the former aspired to the status of the latter.

On this matter, as on so many others, Gough Whitlam was ahead of his time. Not for him the hackneyed opening to an address: Ladies and Gentlemen. He always began with a resounding 'Men and Women of Australia'.

I hope that nothing I've said is interpreted to mean that, while 'lady' deserves the axe, 'gentleman' should be spared.

It is tarred with the same brush, in fact it has even less claim on survival. I like to think we are moving into a historical stage where there will be no special place for ladies or gentlemen – in word or in deed.

18 June 1988

THE MENACE
THAT STALKS OUR LANGUAGE

We must keep our gaze fixed firmly on the big picture, never missing a window of opportunity for maintaining a level playing field while interfacing with the right models and taking on board a methodology which will provide a basket of options for photo opportunities to demonstrate that the bottom line of the main game will soon be on the table.

O language of Shakespeare and Milton, hast thou fled this Earth forever?

Perhaps the only way to stem the tidal wave of jargon is for voters to write to their local members of Parliament, State and Federal, informing them that they will not vote for them next time around unless they sign a pledge – and adhere to it – never again to use any of the terms mentioned above.

For it is the politicians of all parties who are leading the charge against our beautiful mother tongue. The chief offender is Paul Keating, who loves jargon much more dearly than he loves people.

We have also a Prime Minister who loves sporting heroes more than he loves Labor principles. So it is natural that the cliché 'the level playing field' should hold special appeal for him. By the way, when our current crop of pollies use this expression it usually means not the fair go for all which it is supposed to suggest but another bit of deregulation to clear obstacles from the path of the robber barons who are their role-models. (There I go, falling into the trap myself. That is the worst of jargon. It is like a virus from which nobody is immune.)

Our politicians need reminding that there have been great orators, such as Menzies and Whitlam, who could make stirring speeches without resort to any of the jargon which clutters and defaces the modern political vocabulary.

It would be easy to dismiss jargon as a harmless, passing fad. In the mouths of politicians and lackeys, including the commentators who pamper their egos by publishing and magnifying the significance of their every word, it has a perhaps unconscious but nonetheless sinister purpose. They hope that it will clothe them with the raiment of the insider, the possessor of arcane insights, the purveyor of specialist solutions beyond the comprehension of the mob. More often they are a camouflage for their own banality.

The real experts in jargon are the lawyers and they too have a sinister intent. By using language that the layperson does not understand, they enhance their image as occupants of a higher realm of knowledge to which the ordinary man and woman cannot aspire. Like their absurd medieval garb, it contributes to the mystique of their calling and helps them get away with the extravagant price of their services.

This is not an argument against the unceasing fertilisation and organic growth of our language. English did not spring whole from the head of Zeus. It has gradually evolved, enriched by words adopted from other tongues, by words which may have had their origin in the gutter but turn out to be more apt to describe a phenomenon or experience than more highfalutin' terms, by words which come into being to fit new concepts and discoveries, and by the inventions of imaginative writers.

Words and combinations of words go through a Darwinian process of survival of the fittest. Some don't make the grade and just drop out of usage. They may survive in the dictionaries like the full *Oxford English Dictionary* but they are like the human appendix, present but not used. Perhaps I will be proved wrong and some of the modern political jargon will pass the only test that matters: usage. But, in my view, most of it deserves to wither on the vine and politicians will be driven back to reliance on a source which provides a rich, varied and colourful store of words in which to express their thoughts: the English language.

If I may be permitted to switch to a more serious subject, my eye was caught recently by a letter on the letters page of this paper from a 17-year-old girl. It was a *cri de coeur* from much put-upon youth protesting against the contumely which is heaped upon their generation by a previous generation which has bequeathed to them a world with defacements such as the danger of nuclear destruction, an ecosystem so threatened as to endanger future existence on this planet, AIDS and the enshrinement of the god Greed.

My heart went out to this young woman and, even though I recalled that when I was her age I was thrown on to the labour market at a moment of widespread human despair in the middle of the Great Depression, the outlook of thinking youth today must also be clouded by the darkest forebodings.

The best advice I can give them is: study history. It may be presumptuous of me to offer advice to the young, since despair for the future of humankind is one of the self-indulgences of the old. H. G. Wells, who spent a long life trumpeting the wonders and liberating influence of science, wrote in his eighties a despairing book *Mind at the End of Its Tether*.

But another great intellectual, the American historian Barbara Tuchman, more recently wrote a book, *A Distant Mirror*, which is a scholarly, compassionate account of one of the most awful centuries through which our species has lived, the fourteenth.

That was the century of the Great Plague which wiped out an enormous percentage of the world's then relatively small population, and of incessant, pointless warfare. It is hard to imagine a century, before ours, in which the doom of the species seemed more probable. But humankind survived, by the skin of its teeth.

Don't despair, young people. Man is a resilient creature, woman even more so.

27 April 1989

MATESHIP CAN PROVE FATAL

Every now and then a little applause encourages me to continue the outpourings which in some other circles may provoke hopes of my imminent demise.

In a piece I penned recently which was a little less than adulatory of Rhodes Scholars I had met, I made an exception of one of their number who had charmed everyone who knew or read him. He was Ross Campbell, the wittiest Australian columnist I can remember, who finally put down his pen a couple of years ago.

A reader who approved my remarks turned out to be a Ross Campbell fan also and he enclosed a photocopy of one of Ross's best pieces. (For the benefit of aficionados, it appeared in the *Bulletin* of 19 December 1970.)

The theme was the overuse of the term 'mate'. He pointed out, in his usual droll style, that it was often a grave mistake for the recipient of such a greeting to mistake it as a declaration of friendship.

In support of this warning he cited an incident in which a truck driver had shouted: 'Why don't you learn to drive, mate.' Some of us have shared that experience.

Now Ross was much too delightful a man ever to stray anywhere near politics. If he had, he would have learnt that without the word 'mate' politicians just could not ply their trade. They would be like a carpenter without a hammer.

The word is the indispensable fill-in while you are groping

13

around for the name to attach to the face of a beaming admirer who accosts you with outstretched hand in the confident belief that his/her name is engraved on your memory. You push all the buttons, but the old cranial computer does not respond.

In my brief sojourn in the groves of the philosopher-kings, one of my colleagues in the Senate invariably gave an Oscar-winning performance on such occasions. His standard salutation was: 'Good to see you, mate', spoken with a glowing sincerity which would have been believable only if he were greeting Marilyn Monroe or Sophia Loren.

The fallibility of human memory is one of the many galling aspects of being a politician. When you are on the game you meet many people, often on the wing, so to speak. Even the most illustrious of politicians enjoys no immunity from this occupational pitfall.

There is a story of Dr H. V. Evatt at an annual meeting of the faithful of his electorate walking around a large room along a line of handshakers. Just as the Queen or Prince Charles, nudged by a well-briefed minder, may occasionally pause for a chat with an identified notable or even a carefully selected nonentity, the Doc came to a halt before a face in the crowd and asked: 'How's your father?' in the caring tone which most politicians are able to summon up.

The old party man replied: 'I'm sorry to have to tell you, Doc, that since you were last here Dad has passed away.'

After the appropriate commiserations the Doc proceeded and in due course came face to face again with the same constituent. A triggering mechanism brought the same question to his lips: 'How's your father?'

This time there was a note of acerbity in the reply: 'Still dead.'

Little has changed since Ross wrote his piece. He mentions that 'mate' may often have sinister connotations as in the newspaper account of the time (which was probably imaginary): 'A pack of skinheads viciously slashed a man eight times with cut-throat razors in a lane at Crows Nest last night. "You're going to die, mate," the gang told their victim as their razors sliced into his arms, chest and face.'

Years later, Bill Hayden was to recall that while his political blood was being spilled by his own party's hatchetmen, one of the leaders of the skinheads of that party who was settling his fate, kept 'mating' him in the process. Since then Graham Richardson (now blow-waved) has been called to a peak which anyone who knew him then would have thought well beyond his reach. It just shows that political climbing involves the judicious use of the word 'mate'.

While we are indulging in this semantic byplay, may I have leave to refer to another habit of some of our most exposed politicians of calling their interviewers by their first name. 'Funny you should ask, Richard', or 'That's an interesting way to put it, Max', or 'Now just a moment, Laurie'. Or more sharply to a well-known burr under the saddle: 'That's a stupid question, Alan.'

One wonders what would happen if any of them presumed to call him 'Bob' on air. Surely their public eschewal of such an assertion of intimacy entitles interviewers to reciprocal treatment, instead of the patronising flattery which implies: 'You be nice to me and I'll be nice to you.'

A talented and probing interviewer who shall remain nameless told me that she always winces if, in the course of an interview, she is called 'Jane'.

Although I have often been on reasonably close personal terms with an interviewer, I adjudged it to be in bad taste to presume in any way on our personal relationship in a professional situation.

Early in my political career, I remember complimenting Max Walsh on a particularly sharp hatchet job he had done on a politician who was not one of my favourites. While accepting my compliments Max remarked: 'Don't worry. If you do something I don't like, you'll get the same treatment.'

That's as it should be. Mateship has no place in the professional relationships between politicians and the media.

29 February 1988

15

A NEW KIND OF STIGMATISM

I'd like to enter a mild protest against 'ismism'. I'm pretty sure the word has already surfaced but, if not, it deserves a place in any worthwhile lexicon of modern usage.

First, let me proffer a tentative definition: 'ismism' is the tendency to brand as evidence of ingrained and irrational prejudice any criticism, however mild, of certain (real or imagined) threatened species; for example blacks, women, Jews, small people, old people, cats and dogs.

That list is not exhaustive but it will suffice to illustrate my point. The commonest isms are racism, sexism and anti-Semitism, but words can be found for the others I have mentioned, such as sizeism, ageism, anti-felinism and anti-caninism.

So, an ismist is one who has isms on the brain.

I don't go all the way with Winston Churchill's observation that all the isms had become wasisms. Some, I fear, will always be with us. The language that got Sydney broadcaster Ron Casey the sack (although his non-parole period has been reduced) can justly be described as racist, in his case denoting an irrational prejudice against Asians.

Ismism in its most virulent form implies that there are people or animals or institutions that are above criticism and that those who break that taboo deserve to be lumped in with Casey and Ruxton and their ilk.

In a recent issue of the *Good Weekend*, the *Herald*'s New York correspondent, Paul Sheehan, pointed out that he would be crossing the invisible line of media don'ts if he were to report in any respectable American newspaper or magazine the (true) story that Jesse Jackson is a man with frightening and potentially dangerous demagogic tendencies, or to remind readers that

Jackson had once referred to New York as 'Hymietown', that a public audit had disclosed that $US1 million ($1.23 million) was missing from his lobbying group's fund and that he is a fast-talking, self-aggrandising con artist. (He might have added that Jackson claimed that Martin Luther King had died in his arms, when Jackson was nowhere near the death scene.)

Any white who criticises a black is expected to prove that his criticism is not based on colour. Unlike so many white people, there are evidently no awful black people.

I have often been called a pro-Semite because of my genuine admiration for the Jewish people. But I was recently accused of anti-Semitism for voicing some reservations about the way the Israelis were coping with the disorders of the Left Bank. I replied by pointing out that there are divisions on the subject within the Israeli Government and that I have heard far harsher criticisms than mine of Israeli behaviour from other Jewish people.

Anyhow, aren't friends allowed to criticise friends? I once referred to a person I did not admire as 'that dreadful little bastard'. One of my closest friends, himself a small man and a considerable wit, laughingly rebuked me for sizeism.

I also claim to have made some progress in shedding the sexism that I and almost all of my generation (along with many subsequent generations) imbibed with my mother's milk. But I was severely taken to task by an ardent feminist for using the generic term 'mankind'. It proved to her that I was really still an unreconstructed sexist.

As for ageism, or contempt for the old, since this is an ism of which I am frequently on the receiving end, I can assure those who hold age against me that the water runs straight off this old drake's back when I hear that I have been referred to as 'that dreadful old bastard'. After all, you are only old once, and it is preferable to the alternative.

But a person I very much admire, folk-singer Eric Bogle, told me recently that he, a cat lover all his life, had been falsely accused of anti-felinism. Why? For writing and singing a mock-tragic but affectionate little ditty called *You're Nobody's Moggie*

Now, about a cat that picked an unsuccessful fight with a truck, the result of which we have all seen on almost any public highway.

Recently, there has been quite a bit of discussion in the media of the problem created by the natural human tendency to take dogs for a walk and the natural canine tendency to defecate away from their home ground. I dare say that, in some fanatical circles, anybody who suggested that some solution should be found to the resultant problem of people treading in dog's poo and then walking it into the Persian carpet was an anti-caninist.

As Shakespeare (who was himself a dab hand at inventing words) might have said, if the word had been around in his day: 'Thus ismism doth make cowards of us all.' It inhibits the free flow of conversation by making us suppress comments that are not based on any real prejudice, and fosters a lot of verbal pussyfooting, just as our repressive laws of defamation make for dull journalism.

Ismism is itself irrational and anti-intellectual, since it fosters illusions of a world that does not exist. It *is* possible for some blacks to be evil, it *is* possible for some women to be less than perfect, it *is* possible for a Jewish government sometimes to act just like any other government – badly.

These days, for reasons of encroaching senility, I immediately forget the names of people to whom I am introduced. There is an attractive and intelligent black woman whom I have met on a few social occasions who is only one of the victims of my amnesia.

When I enter a crowded room and see her among the throng, I duck for cover because I know that, if I greet her without calling her by name, she will be reinforced in the view she obviously holds of me, that I am a racist sexist.

And, when she notices me dodging her, as she invariably does, she signals by a less-than-friendly glance that she is more convinced than ever that she's got me summed up.

Actually, I like her. See what I mean?

1 August 1988

18

AN INFALLIBLE GUIDE TO UNSAFE CONVERSATION AND BETTER DINNER PARTIES

It has long been considered that the safest subject of conversation was the weather, regarding which you may usually count on a consensus between men and women, old and young, conservatives and radicals, Catholics and Protestants.

But even the weather has become a conversational minefield. I recently raised the matter of the exceptionally mild winter of 1988, only to run into a tirade from a young environmentalist about the 'greenhouse effect'.

This experience prompted a few thoughts about the perils of conversation.

That is a shadow which hangs over any gathering of people at any time of the year. But the dangers are exacerbated during the silly season which, mercifully, does not last forever (around about Australia Day is the usual cut-off point). It is a time when there is more leisure and party-going than usual and conversation must take its place among the peculiarly seasonal perils such as skin cancer, liver damage, insufferable TV and cricket, cricket, cricket.

Once upon a time there was an unspoken convention called Safe Conversation, the rules of which applied especially at polite dinner parties. The taboo subjects were Sex, Politics and Religion. I can remember being invited to dinner by a well-known and extremely conservative citizen who had decided that, for a Labor man, I was comparatively civilised.

As we sat down to dinner and I gazed around the table I felt like a member of an endangered species. I was placed next to my host's wife, a vivacious, bird-like creature who twittered rather than talked.

To many people conversation is not an opportunity to exchange information and opinions, let alone to sing for your supper with the occasional witty interpolation, but merely a device to avoid that worst of all social catastrophes, silence.

A lot of people who have a lot to say don't have much to talk about. My hostess fell into that category, but after a while it seemed to dawn on her that I was somewhat less than spellbound by her chirpings. So she decided, evidently because she dimly recalled having been told that I was a politician, to try politics.

If, up to that point, she had shown little acquaintance with anything that even vaguely interested me, her knowledge of politics did not extend beyond regarding it as a game of goodies (her lot) and baddies (the rest). Suddenly there was one of those lulls in the general shouting which bedevil even the best-managed dinner parties, through which his wife's inanities drifted to the host at the other end of the table.

Whereupon he rose and wagged an admonitory finger: 'Mirabelle,' (I'm trying to avoid identification) he thundered, only half-jokingly, 'didn't I warn you to lay off politics with Jim?'

Whereupon Mirabelle switched to flower arrangement. This illustrates the dangers of having a conversational blacklist. For most people, if you bar Sex, Politics and Religion you leave them with nothing to talk about.

One of the best examples of the perils of conversation which comes to mind is a story by James Thurber of a couple, married for many years, who go to a film starring Greta Garbo.

On returning home after the film the wife advances the proposition that Greta Garbo is the greatest screen star of all times. The husband dissents, mildly at first, but the wife persists stridently in upholding her choice and challenges him to name a superior to the scrumptious Swede.

He volunteers the name of Donald Duck. As she pours scorn and derision on this choice, the argument hots up to such a temperature that he packs up, walks out and spends the night at his club. And that was the end of the marriage.

The point of that story, of course, is that a relationship can turn so sour that almost anything can make it curdle. However, I have a long-standing and cherished friend to whom, at a certain stage of lubrication, the most casual throwaway line can serve as the trigger for a verbal brawl.

When I used to see such a mood coming on, I could not resist baiting him further. But as we have both become older and less excitable the steam has gone out of our conversational imbroglios.

One rule of conversation which should be borne in mind when you are floundering around searching for a subject is illustrated by a little anecdote told to me recently by the wife of a political friend.

She told me that she had found herself at several political dinners seated next to a certain Great Man who shall remain nameless.

Being an outgoing type who enjoys good talk and quite a wit, she would try to get a conversation going but the Great Man showed few conversational gifts and did little to conceal his boredom.

Finally, one evening as she was on the point of despair at the prospects of the *longueurs* of the meal ahead, she had an inspiration: I'll try talking to him about him.

Eureka! The conversation which ensued never flagged for a moment. At last she had found the key to his interest. So bear that in mind, dear readers. Few of us fail to be beguiled by a touching interest in our own splendid and unique selves. The flatterer is seldom interrupted.

There is nothing wrong with a touch of malice in conversation and in any event it is ineradicable. I used to think lawyers were the most bitchy until I got to know a few architects. And journos hold their own in any company. So long as you recognise that some group in another corner will be busy frying you while you are roasting them, malice is to be valued as the mustard of conversation.

The only unforgivable conversational sin is boring people. So, disregarding the failures of all previous conversational blacklists, I propose a new list of barred topics: the superiority of Sydney over Melbourne and vice versa; the superiority of private over public education and vice versa; and the most heinous of all: what I got for my old house and what I paid for my new one.

19 January 1989

Notes for would-be authors

So you want to be a famous author? Well, writing the book is the easy part. It is after your masterpiece gets into the hands of your publisher that your troubles begin.

'Yes, it's great, couldn't put it down. There are just a few little things we'd like to suggest. We'll be assigning an editor who'll get in touch with you and make a few suggestions.'

The editor assigned to me was Irina Dunn, before she became senator. I have no complaints about Irina except that she made me work so hard after I'd thought the knock-off whistle had gone. I had to write extra chapters and replace all the 'mankinds' with 'humankinds' to get rid of what she called my unconscious sexism.

And then, after being so proud of my title, I had to select another to satisfy my publisher. Fortunately my wife relieved me of that chore by coming up with a better one than that which I had chosen. So it became *Stirring the Possum*.

After you've finished the book you feel something like I imagine a mother must feel after she has squeezed her offspring out into the world: well, at last I've got that out of my system.

But the analogy with motherhood is closer than I had imagined. You've then got to suckle the brat. First of all, there's the launch. I have been to many a launch and at least I can say that my publisher turned on something better to drink than that cask stuff that I call 'launch wine'. My friend John Button risked demotion to Minister for Trivial Pursuits by doing the launch for a book which is not overly kind to some of his confrères.

It is about this time that writer's paranoia sets in. You gaze around at the faces of your friends and the sprinkling of enemies and you see more of the latter and you realise that your offspring is being launched into a tough world. You begin to realise, too, the significance of the old imprecation: Oh, that my enemy would write a book!

From then on you become a cross between a profound thinker and a performing seal, in short a media pundit. I had to run the gamut of the electronic media of all States (except Queensland, where it was evidently adjudged that nothing could compete with the greatest show on Earth, the Fitzgerald Inquiry).

This involved being put on hold, sometimes for as long as ten minutes, while the radio interviewer played a few commercial jingles to which you had to listen before the time came for you to perform for the public.

The quality of interviewing in this country is variable, especially about anything serious. And what could be more serious than *your* contribution to the history of your times?

My interviewers were mostly intelligent and I even got the impression that some of them had read the book. One wet Melbourne day, as I was whisked around the city from one radio station to another to meet a schedule drawn up for an athlete rather than a geriatric, I wondered whether the real writers like Peter Carey or Salman Rushdie are submitted to such an ordeal or whether it is reserved for chancy writers from whom publishers are worried about getting their money back.

I fear there is something of an attitude on the part of publishers: we took the risk of publishing your bloody book – the least you can do is to get out and flog it.

Meanwhile you are waiting nervously for the reviews to appear in the print media. I gradually became aware that the sort of reviews that you get don't depend primarily on the quality of your book but on the skills of literary editors in choosing your reviewers.

The fact that I write a column for the Fairfax press certainly earned me no mercy from their publications. I congratulate the literary editors of the *Australian Financial Review* and the *Sydney Morning Herald* on their uncanny choices of reviewers whose toes would have been made most sore by a few brickbats which fell from my pages.

But, of course, no writer is entitled to mercy, least of all myself. If you live by the sword, you must be prepared to perish by the sword. And there were some surprises among my reviews. Clyde Cameron, who became a temporary enemy of mine when Gough Whitlam took the job of Minister for Labour from him and gave it to me in 1975, wrote a magnanimous and adulatory review in the Melbourne *Herald* and Don Dunstan, whose own auto-biography I reviewed rather severely a few years ago, was most kind to my book in the *Bulletin*.

My odyssey finished up in Hobart as guest speaker at the Hobart *Mercury* Literary Lunch held, ironically, in the same room at Wrest Point Convention Centre where the Labor Party holds its national conventions.

As I savoured the gourmet delights of such functions and chatted with the *Mercury*'s editor, I suddenly realised that I was having a free lunch on Rupert Murdoch, the paper's proprietor.

This moved me to tell the editor of the only other lunch the great man had bestowed on me. It was in 1977 in New York when I was a parliamentary delegate to the annual talkfest of the United Nations General Assembly.

For some obscure reason Murdoch, who was then in New York setting up his empire, sought me out and took me, at his suggestion, to a restaurant which looked very much like a McDonald's to me. 'I don't suppose you want any wine?' he asked as I chose the only item on the menu which struck me as nearly edible, a hamburger. I said that I would like some and he ordered a house white for me. The bill was $26.50. I then accompanied him and his wife to a Woody Allen film and he allowed me to buy the tickets for $31.50. It was my first lesson in the ways of tycoons.

For those unkind enough to construe this piece as a commercial, let me hasten to add that there is not much point in advertising a product which is not on the shelves. My publishers were not very generous in assessing the book's saleability as a hardback and even while I was trying to flog it, it was practically unprocurable.

But at least I will not provide the gratification expressed in Clive James's hilarious poem: 'The book of my enemy has been remaindered.'

7 December 1988

LOSING THE MANUSCRIPT

What if Tolstoy had composed *War and Peace* on a computer instead of using his laborious longhand? This thought occurred to me recently on a tour, under the guidance of senior staff, of the State Library of NSW – my first visit since the Macquarie Street wing was officially opened in May last year.

In my student days I haunted the old Mitchell Library, gossiped with fellow students on the steps facing the Botanic Gardens while admiring the girls in their summer dresses, and sometimes ate my lunchtime sandwiches on a seat in adjoining Figtree Avenue, now absorbed in the freeway linking the Cahill Expressway with Woolloomooloo and sporting only a few, sad, truncated remnants of its once-magnificent Moreton Bay figs.

The State Library has come a long way since then and is now one of Sydney's greatest treasures, rating as one of the best services of its kind in the world. The Mitchell Library is a major national research collection of resources relating to Australia, the South-West Pacific and Antarctica.

That over-familiar and yawnsome term, the 'Bicentennial Project', at least finds worthy expression in the new Macquarie Street wing. Designed by Andrew Andersons, formerly assistant government architect, it is linked to the 'old' library by two walkways, one underground from the Mitchell reading room to level seven of the Macquarie Street wing and one in the form of an enclosed bridge from the exhibition galleries of the Mitchell to level nine of the new wing.

As you enter the new building from Macquarie Street, it comes as a shock to realise that you are on level eight of that building. Seven floors are in the bowels of the earth. But that is an inspired idea, since there is no functional reason why the five storage floors for the two floors of the general reference library should be above ground; and by confining the visual portion to two levels, the harmony of this section of the Macquarie streetscape is preserved.

The nucleus of the Mitchell Library is David Scott Mitchell's personal collection of 61 000 printed volumes, and thousands of maps, manuscripts and papers.

Mitchell (1836–1907), an early graduate of Sydney University, was a reclusive bachelor who devoted the last thirty years of his life to building up the finest collection of Australian material in the world. He bequeathed his collection, with a substantial endowment for its maintenance, to the Public Library of NSW, but with the proviso that within a year of his death the Government must erect a suitable building to house it. The present building was begun in 1906 and completed in 1910.

So what have Tolstoy and computers to do with all this? Accompany me to the archives section of the library complex and you will find out.

For my special delectation, the staff had extracted some of their manuscript treasures. There is a particular *frisson* for lovers of language in looking at the physical product of the thoughts of famous people perpetuated on paper at the moment of its birth. I doubt whether there is as much joy to be had from gazing at a floppy disc, which will be all that archivists of the future will have to show students of those whose creative efforts went straight into a computer.

I was shown the letter written by poor old Henry Lawson, part-time literary figure and full-time drunk, penned from Darlinghurst Jail, uncomplaining and philosophical; also his will, brief and written in pencil, as befits a man who has almost nothing material to bequeath.

There are treasures here for students of trade union history, as there are rich collections of trade union minutes, all handwritten and remarkably legible. Ever since I have been attending meetings – political, union or whatever – it has been somebody's job to 'type up the minutes' from rough notes taken contemporaneously. In earlier times, they used to write them up. After looking at these minute books I wondered if the ability to write exquisite copperplate was a mandatory qualification for all 'writers-up' of minutes.

Among the most interesting of the documents to be found in the Mitchell archives is the foundation minute book, dated 1920–21, of the Communist Party of Australia. I glanced through it and was delighted to find a reference to Guido Baracchi, one of its founding fathers and later one of the many who fell from grace and was expelled for 'deviationism', or some such heinous offence. I knew him in his closing years, when he was infected with what his co-founding fathers would have regarded as the leprosy of Trotskyism.

But perhaps the most striking manuscript that was shown to me was Bligh's journal, written with total legibility and embellished with highly skilful sketches of coastline topography, all in Bligh's own hand, during his astonishing journey from Tahiti to Timor in the open boat in which he and his officers had been cast adrift by the Bounty mutineers. As if the feat of navigating such a vessel over a journey of more than 6000 kilometres was not enough!

Ever since I saw a photostat of a page of Proust's manuscript of *A la Recherche du Temps Perdu*, with its balloons of interpolations into the already labyrinthine sentences, I have appreciated what an original manuscript has to tell us of the creative process.

But, watching the skilled word–processor operators (whose ranks I fear I will never join) expunge all traces of discarded formulations and move words, sentences and whole paragraphs from one position to another merely by pressing a key or two, I've realised that future records of the birth of masterpieces may foster an impression that they sprang whole from the head of Zeus.

This is not a Luddite plea to smash our computers, the greatest technological breakthrough since James Watt's discovery of the uses of steam; it is merely a reminder that with every scientific gain something is also lost.

4 January 1989

SHOCK, HORROR . . .
LABOR LEFTIES IN DIRTY DEALS

If the recent Federal conference of the ALP proved anything, it was the need for a new dictionary of political terminology.

What is left of the Left? Is the Right any more clearly defined when it calls itself Centre Unity? Does Centre Left mean anything more than a distaste for both of the traditional factions allied to a recognition that, in practice, you have to do business with them or wash your hands of the dirty game of politics?

The decay of the meaning of labels inside the ALP merely reflects the general semantic obfuscation of political discussion by the use of terms appropriate to an era which has long passed and an economy which has become a museum piece.

Do capitalist or socialist or conservative or liberal (or Democrat) help in any way to define what people or parties sailing under such colours stand for?

The reporting of the conference by the media showed that journalists, with a few notable exceptions, continue to be prisoners of words which have long lost any power to describe what is happening in the real world of politics.

The most pungent and clear-sighted comment on the proceedings came, in my view, from the *Australian Financial Review*'s columnist, David Clark, who wrote: 'There is little more to the ALP national conference than a series of dirty deals in assorted bedrooms between ex-Communist Party union officials and the old Catholic Right of the party.'

This was a reference to the deal cooked up between such unlikely allies as the Stalinist apostate, John Halfpenny, and the Tammany Catholic archetype, John MacBean, to attempt to breathe life into the corpse of protectionism and to clip the wings of the Government's brightest and best performer, John Button. Fortunately he did them like a dinner. That deal signalled to me the imminent demise of the so-called Left.

One of the great political confidence tricks has been the aura of doctrinal purity and moral superiority with which the Left's propagandists have managed to surround their faction. They have been for socialism (whatever that may mean), they have been against opportunism (now called pragmatism) and, above all, even though some of them are nominal Catholics, they have been against the politics of Catholicism.

It has never been sufficiently recognised that factionalism in the ALP has much less to do with ideology than with preselection. An aspiring politician sniffs the wind in the branches which decide his fate and trims his sails accordingly.

But being an accredited leftie evidently confers no immunity to the contagion of pragmatism. The deal between Halfpenny and MacBean disclosed that economic primitivism, pragmatism and plain opportunism (posturing before their members as defenders of their jobs) are more powerful than any of the ideological differences which are supposed to divide the factions.

How many people in any faction of the ALP believe any more in socialism, which still gets many a ritualistic obeisance in the official platform? I am reminded of the Biblical saw: 'In the beginning was the Word, and the Word was with God, and the Word was God.' I have never understood what the cabbalistic sentence was supposed to mean, but I suspect that its very inscrutability has contributed to its acceptance by the fundamentalists.

The same goes for socialism. Its indefinability invites genuflection. It is like the common reply to the question whether you believe in God: you have to have something to believe in.

To question the efficacy or relevance of the socialist banner to rally the growing number of people disaffected with the status quo to a program of change is not to abandon the need for change. But what we are talking about here is not aims but the words in which those aims are expressed.

If there is one point on which believing socialists could hitherto be pinned down, it was on the need to regulate the economy rather than leave it at the mercy of people with money whose only aim is to make more money.

The deregulation of our financial system sponsored by Paul Keating amounts to a definitive abandonment of that central socialist tenet. History may prove him right, although I notice that doubts are being expressed about its viability among the international financial moguls, who seem to be contemplating the need to return to regulation.

But if deregulation sticks, it amounts to a requiem for socialism. So, if the Left still believed in socialism, it would have waged the greatest fight in the history of the ALP on this question. But all we heard were a few timid squeaks of dissent. After that, what's left of the Left? They have ceded the pass without a fight.

Stepping into the wider arena, what is today's contest about between the two major political groupings? Has it got anything to do with the redistribution downwards of national wealth?

In the Keating era, Labor's claim on the electorate's support is based on nothing more than an assertion of superior skill in maintaining an unchallenged private enterprise system as a going concern.

There are marginal differences between the ALP and the Liberals as to the desirable level of welfare spending, and on the part of the Liberals a sprinkling of the icing sugar of privatisation on the stodgy suet pudding which they proffer to the electors. But, basically, Hawke and Howard are Tweedledum and Tweedledee, who compete only in the banality of their salesmanship.

What else is on offer in the political market? The communists have all but disappeared and the Trotskyists, as they have always been, are no more than an irrelevant ratbag sect.

True, on the far Right we have the neo-conservatives. But this tiny group of New York intellectuals, centred around Irving Kristol and Norman Podhoretz, is merely dishing up a sophisticated version of Johism. The latter has a regular column in the *Australian*, but if you've read one, you've read them all. The usual paraphernalia of red-neckery (anti-abortion, anti-homosexuality) is regularly paraded, but the overriding message is that Reagan is a saint and Gorbachev is a devil.

The group undoubtedly has a few adherents here, centred around the *Quadrant* crowd, but it is, and I guess it will remain, on the margin of politics, supplying stylishly phrased arguments for the most reactionary policies. It all adds up to old garbage in new pails. Incidentally, while we are on the question of a change to meaningful political nomenclature, I suggest they be renamed the Ameromaniacs.

Since I joined the Labor Party back in the far-distant 1940s, the world has changed and is still changing so fast that we are all lagging behind reality and describing it in outmoded language.

The terms Left, Right and Centre derived their original political use from the seating of the various parties in the French National Assembly after the Revolution of 1789. The others – capitalist, communist, liberal, conservative – are early nineteenth-century terms.

As to the trade unions, the absurdity of continuing to regard them merely as organisations for the defence of their members against employers is illustrated by the Halfpenny–MacBean deal, which has exposed their major role today to be an attempt to halt the decline of industries which have lost the right to exist in their present condition.

The other day Barrie Unsworth dashed hopes that he might be a forward-looking politician by expressing a wistful longing for a return to the values of the 1950s. He has been alive long enough to realise that the good old days never existed and, in any event, that you can't bring them back.

We live in harsh times and, if we are to believe the pundits, they will get worse. My humble contribution to the daunting tasks ahead is to suggest that we should start to call people and parties by names which illuminate rather than obscure what they are on about, starting with the Left. I appeal to journalists to excise that word from their political vocabulary.

15 July 1986

TURNING LABOR INTO A DESIGNER LABEL

I have read somewhere that residents in the outer suburbs of Leningrad (then called Petrograd, and before that St Petersburg) didn't know anything unusual was happening at the time the angry masses were storming the Winter Palace in the centre of the city.

The October Revolution did not interrupt their quotidian round.

Communications are so instantaneous today that it's hard to imagine a modern equivalent of such imperviousness to history in the making. It would be something like the good burghers of Wahroonga not knowing there was an armed insurrection going on in Martin Place.

But when the three delegates of Young Labor walked out of last week's Labor conference while the Prime Minister was pontificating, to show their indignation over what they perceived to be happening to their party, they were unconsciously demonstrating a not very dissimilar blindness to historical changes which have been occurring for some time under their very noses.

The Labor Party to which they thought they belonged may have undergone its ritual burial at Hobart, but its death throes should have been obvious for at least the past three years.

There is no law of history which dictates that political parties last for ever. Several have disappeared in our short history. Remember the DLP?

Parties are born out of social and economic circumstances, like the Labor Party in the nineties of the past century. As times change, it is in the nature of things that parties change too, and even disappear. Confusion arises only when the names have not been changed, to protect the innocent.

The charge that should be levelled against those who call the tune in today's Labor Party should not be of betrayal of principle, but of trading under a false label.

The party should change its name and forget all about pursuing its lost constituency. It now has a different constituency which could well keep electing it for as long as the voters continued to elect Menzies. What else is politics all about? The ALP should drop all pretence of being the party of the working class.

The founder and Pope of the new party is Paul Keating. I should like to make it clear that the purpose of this article is not to condemn him or his theology. I am merely advocating a correction in political terminology.

In an off-the-cuff aside, during one of his last speeches in the recently concluded session of Parliament, he launched into the most brilliant critique of conservative political performance in this country which I have heard. It was characteristically vituperative, but it was a profound analysis of the bankruptcy of conservative political philosophy and practice in Australia over the past fifty years.

The significant feature of the speech was that it did not attack the conservatives for callousness or indifference to the condition of the ordinary man and woman – the stock rhetoric of Labor politicians down the ages. The gravamen of his attack was their ineptitude, their lack of understanding of their own system and their consequential failure to take the necessary steps to avert our present plight.

I understand how a market economy works, he asserted, and I am running this economy in the way it should be run. Of course he said 'we' instead of 'I', but you had to be a political babe in arms to miss his message. He doesn't think anybody else in his Party has his grip on economic reality.

The ascendancy which Keating has achieved over his party is not only due to having more brains than the others, but also to the fact that much of his critique of what the traditional Labor Party has regarded as gospel is correct. He has been too politically astute to buy into the privatisation brawl, knowing that fidelity to public ownership is the last vestigial trace of the 'socialist objective', and thus, an icon to which lip service must be paid even by those who have long lost the faith.

To many Laborites, it's like not being able to bring yourself to declare a disbelief in God even though you've given up going to church.

But when Keating gets the top job, as he inevitably will, just watch how few public enterprises survive.

An even greater gift of Keating's is his ability to build around himself an aura of infallibility and to portray those who disagree with him as sentimental, backward-looking fossils.

Keating argues, correctly, that the end of the grand illusion that our commodity exports would always finance our imports, and that we could afford a self-indulgent manufacturing industry immunised from the chill winds of competition, dictates a change of direction in the management of our economy.

But I do not agree that recognition of that reality also involves retention of a taxation system which favours the affluent; a benign acceptance, indeed encouragement, of growing mono-polisation by spivvy entrepreneurs, especially in the commun-ications industry; and a tertiary education policy which penalises people for getting a degree.

While I accept the inevitability of Keating's ascension to the throne, I would like to see his infallibility successfully challenged on the matter of next year's projected adjustment of the taxation scale.

I belong to an income bracket which would be advantaged by a reduction of the top rate to thirty-nine per cent which, on current reports, is what Keating has in mind.

But I do not feel entitled to be relieved of any of my present tax obligations while so many people need government succour in the fields of housing, health and education. Even less deserving of such largesse are those whose incomes are far larger than mine.

This issue will be an interesting test of sincerity of the fast-disappearing Left of the ALP. Few of them are poor and most of them would benefit from a reduction of the top rate.

Peter Walsh, that acerbic slasher of Government spending, is currently carrying the flag for a more equitable progressivity in the tax scale. More power to his arm, especially as he carries less taint of 'wetness' than almost anyone in Parliament.

This issue may be Hawke's last chance to stake a claim to be more 'pro-battler' than the young Pretender. But, in a matter so close to their hearts, would Hawke be able to resist the pressure of his great and powerful friends?

16 June 1988

A MACABRE RITUAL

If it were not as serious as all the shock-horror reactions of the pundits suggest, the December quarter increase in the CPI figures would have a certain aspect of macabre humour.

There has been an increasing ritualisation of Australian political and economic life; the agenda is set by a relatively small bunch of politicians and media pundits who, for much of their time, occupy the same grandiose building in an artificial city immured from the real world.

The health of our society is measured by these authoritative persons according to a series of events in the annual calendar: the August Budget, the May Economic Statement if things are going so badly that we need one, the quarterly CPI figures and the monthly balance of trade figures being the high feast days – or days of mourning – of the year.

We out here in the real world are submitted to a series of

bemusing interpretations of the figures which emerge on these ritual occasions.

The gospel according to these gurus – and the consensus, despite the occasional quibble over minutiae, is quite remarkable – goes something like this:

The worst thing that can happen is a depression. The next worst is a recession, which is really a small depression. Almost as bad is inflation, which is caused by trying to avoid recession. High interest rates increase the problems of home buyers but the alternative is to cut Government spending on things like health, education, welfare and infrastructure items like transport and that is not so much bad in itself as vote-costly. Everybody wants more in the pay packet but it can be afforded for senior executives only. Everybody wants to pay less tax but bigger pay packets (except those for the senior executives) may fuel inflation. And all political parties want to win and hold office but only one can succeed and that's why they must appear to differ about the solution to our problems – which can't be solved anyway.

No wonder, as Ross Gittins pointed out yesterday, that economics is known as the dismal science. But somebody always seems to be able to make a profit out of disaster.

The rise in the value of the dollar and the immediate increase in both short- and long-term interest rates occasioned by the CPI rise indicate that the money-market boys are in for their pickings. And, as Keating appears to concede, they are the ones whose reactions to economic events count most.

The most bizarre reactions to the latest bad news have come from the Prime Minister and the Treasurer, and can be summed up as 'shoot the messenger'.

If the CPI figures are so bad, it's because the Statistician included in his figures the increases in housing costs and doesn't measure these increases properly. Does the cost of housing have anything to do with the cost of living? Of course not, say our leaders, except for people who want to buy houses. So leave it out and CPI figures will look better, even if people trying to buy houses have to pay so much that most of them can't afford one.

Well, aren't all these rituals becoming a bit tedious? The most tiresome ritual of all is the product of our outmoded Federal system, to which the outgoing Governor-General, Sir Ninian Stephen, recently drew attention. We are witnessing a re-run of that childish game of It's-all-your-fault, No-it's-all-your-fault, so convenient as an alibi for both State and Federal governments.

Isn't it ironical? Our long-festering housing problem looks like getting a guernsey, not because State or Federal governments have suddenly been touched by the plight of people who have been striving desperately and in vain for years to find adequate accommodation for themselves and their families, but because housing costs are making the CPI figures look bad.

If the housing summit of State Premiers and the Federal Government which Paul Keating now proposes comes to pass, it is devoutly to be hoped that the ritualistic name-calling to which we have become accustomed will be avoided and that a serious attempt will be made to come to grips with this problem, which reflects so badly on our claim to be an advanced economy.

One of the contributions which both State and Federal governments will be able to make is the freeing up of valuable land, much of it in areas close to the city centres, which they own and which lie unused, and about which they have so far done nothing but talk.

But they can go further than that. They can address, as no government has hitherto addressed, the urgent need for urban consolidation.

The enormous waste of public money on the provision of infrastructure facilities to service the urban sprawls of our major cities could be materially alleviated by concentrating new housing in the inner suburbs, where a lot of government-owned land is situated.

An abundance of informed advice has been available on this subject to all governments, notably from civic-minded architects and planners like Neville Gruzman and Hugh Stretton.

But governments have not been listening to such voices because they do not belong in the official choir which accompanies the rituals of our polity.

37

What about a bit of lateral thinking, boys and girls? The stage is larger than Canberra; there are ideas and energies to be tapped out here in the real world which just may modify your acceptance of the eternal economic verities which don't seem to be working all that well.

2 February 1989

THE POLITICS OF COMPULSORY VOTING

The expensive propaganda campaign, including full-page advertisements in the metropolitan dailies, urging people 'to give apathy away' and enrol for a vote, which has been conducted by the Federal Government, is worthy of a little scrutiny.

Was it motivated by pure, unsullied devotion to the democratic principle of maximising the exercise of the right to vote, or was there a more political objective?

I make bold to suggest that the thinking behind it was that most of the apathetic, those who have to be urged to exercise their right to vote, will, if they bother to get their names on the roll, be more likely to vote for Labor than for any of the other parties.

The privileged, the educated, the holders of strong opinions can be relied on to vote. They welcome the chance to defend their possessions or their beliefs.

But what of the underprivileged, the two million or so estimated to be living below the poverty line? A lot of them feel anger at their plight and would like to see it improved.

But probably just as many feel merely hopeless and lack faith in amelioration at the hands of any of the political parties.

It has always been an article of faith in Labor circles that those at the bottom of the heap have nowhere else to go but to vote Labor.

38

But first you have to get their names on the roll and then, the thinking goes, the fear of a fine for not voting will make them vote – to the benefit of Labor.

That is why Labor has usually been stronger than non-Labor in its support of compulsory voting. But perhaps their assumptions are beginning to become a little outdated by the changing public perceptions of the role of the traditional parties.

At the time when the 'Joh for Canberra' drive could be taken seriously, there were fears that he might attract some of the many disaffected Labor supporters to his banner because, to the despairing, even snake-oil seems worth a try.

Many of the proletariat (yes, there is still one) vote for Thatcher and many supported Hitler.

This promises to be a most complex election. Howard's tax policy targets certain groups and he tells them unashamedly to vote for him and they'll have more money in their pockets.

Keating's riposte is to tell them that what Howard promises is to give with one hand and take with the other.

How many of those targeted will really be able to discern through the barrage of words of the next four weeks what's really good for them, let alone what's good for the country?

All of this has led me to question my life-long belief in compulsory voting.

It is interesting to reflect on the manner of its birth. In his *Australian National Government* published in 1965, Professor L. F. Crisp wrote:

In 1924 both Houses, without division and with the tacit endorsement of all parties, rapidly passed a Private Member's Bill . . . providing that voting at Federal elections shall be compulsory . . .

It was in fact a Bill desired by both Government and Opposition provided neither could be blamed for its introduction.

Its sponsorship by private members was simply a matter of convenience all round as is evidenced by the fact that it passed through both Houses in the space of 142 minutes without speeches from either Front Bench in either House.

It is suggested that it was introduced not to honour some great democratic principle but as a contrived fix to make life easier for politicians by relieving them of the task of persuading the apathetic to vote at all.

Has it had the effect of making Australia a more democratically governed country than Britain or the US, to whom it has never occurred to adopt it? (You can get government by a minority party in England, not because of the absence of compulsory voting but because of the absence of preferential voting.)

It can be argued that compelling uninterested, reluctant and uninformed people to vote dilutes the value of the votes of serious and well-informed electors by the mass of votes from persons who are voting only because they have to and could not care less about the result.

It has also led to the phenomenon of the donkey vote, the habit of the uninterested elector of voting 1, 2, 3, etc straight down the ballot paper without any regard to the merits of candidate or party.

This has been unscrupulously exploited by parties selecting nonentities because their names start with A or B.

If I may quote Professor Crisp again:

Compulsion seems actually to have discouraged political education by the party.

This has almost certainly helped to make parties lazy between elections about winning this floating vote by propounding a basic political philosophy.

Compulsion also trivialises elections, since the uninterested elector who is compelled to vote is likely to seek the most uncomplicated reason for declaring a preference between the parties, such as Hawke's alleged 'charisma'. What's that got to do with the profound issues of this election?

Though I haven't finally made up my mind about compulsory voting, I no longer regard its alleged merits as self-evident truths.

When the dust settles, perhaps the community might benefit from an informed debate on the subject.

12 June 1987

Let it all hang out

A recent incident in the Federal Parliament, though trivial, raises an interesting question.

I refer to the occasion when John Howard saw fit to reprimand a National Party frontbencher for referring to tapes of a conversation with sexual overtones allegedly involving our accident-prone Minister for Tourism, John Brown.

The incident prompts the question: to what extent are the sexual activities of public figures, either male or female, relevant to their fitness for the offices which they hold or to which they aspire?

Sexual proclivities and preferences, in the widely disparate dimensions of the libido, sexual victories and defeats, are subjects without which literature would be depleted and private conversation flag.

Sex is interesting, funny and unlikely to disappear.

Some famous politicians have been notoriously profligate in their personal lives. But how did that affect their performance of their politicial tasks?

Whatever you may think of his political (as distinct from his sexual) morality, that old satyr Lloyd George rates a little higher on the performance scale than cleaner-than-clean Nancy-doting Ronnie Reagan. The post-mortem disclosures about the sexual lifestyle of that good Catholic President John Kennedy make you wonder how he found time to run the country in between 'scoring' with the most sophomoric absence of discrimination. But he was rated a pretty good president at the time.

Franklin Roosevelt, perhaps the greatest president of them all, was a discreet adulterer. The interesting question in this case is how that wheel-chaired titan managed what comes so easily to most of us. But love, or lust, will find a way.

Why, then, was the disclosure that Gary Hart was an inveterate womaniser, a pursuer of bimbos (to use one of those endearing American terms), fatal to his presidential ambitions?

There are said to have been unspoken deals between the media and Kennedy, Roosevelt, and the famous of those times, that the sexual exploits of the mighty were their own business.

It is an insult to the journalists of those days to imagine that they just did not know what was going on. But, in today's information-hungry era, the competition between the purveyors of news is so intense that those walls of Jericho have crumbled, leaving gaps through which the rampant little voyeuristic gossip writers can scurry and fossick.

The advice which should be heeded by today's public figures is, to vary slightly the Truman philosophy: if you can't stand the heat, stay out of the bedroom.

The sexual habits of a hot gospeller who preaches conjugal fidelity are obviously relevant to his right to hang on to his job. American evangelist Jim Bakker, when exposed as a fornicator, was as much entitled to stay in his post as a bank-teller caught emptying the till into his pocket. Certain prohibitions go with the job.

If I had been a voter in the election which brought Kennedy to power, my assessment of him would have been unaffected by the knowledge that this handsome, privileged young man was not always able to resist the advances of pretty women.

If I had known that he was a systematic, cynical, chauvinist exploiter of the aphrodisiac of power, to whom women were nothing more than points on his score-card, that would have affected my view of his fitness to be America's top banana in one of the most critical periods of its history, even though the alternative was Richard Nixon.

If a female candidate for the American presidency (it could happen) were disclosed to be a man-eating Catherine the Great, that would not disqualify her in my eyes but it is a factor which would weigh in my assessment of her claim to my vote.

I would have to ponder the possibility of some strapping, stupid stud on whom she doted becoming the power behind the throne. (By the way, I'm not suggesting Denis Thatcher runs the United Kingdom. Heaven forfend!)

I hope I have made it clear that I am not a blue-nosed sexual puritan.

But I happen to believe that undiscriminating, promiscuous men or women are unlikely to have the maturity which I consider desirable in aspirants to the governance of our polity.

If John Brown did, in fact, compliment a male journalist on having 'boffed' a female journalist and inquired about the size of her breasts, that is not a matter of earth-shaking significance. It is, lamentably, the way men of all stations talk to each other every day about women.

But I can see no reason why people should not be told what prominent persons are like or have their gaze diverted from the clay feet of the mighty.

In summary, sexual conduct should never be the sole or main determinant in our assessment of aspirants for, or occupants of, high office, as the Fred Niles would like to make it. But such information can be relevant in choosing between Tweedledum and Tweedledee, which is increasingly the choice facing electors.

I'd leave it to the public to weigh up its relevance.

In any event, in no age, in no society, has anybody been able to work out a way of preventing sex getting a public airing.

Today, more than ever, the hungry maw of the media inexorably demands all the fodder which is available. Whether the mighty like it or not, the increasing tendency is to let it all hang out.

25 November 1987

43

HELPMANN'S GAY TIMES

Some of my best friends are gay. I have long had some hesitation in adopting the word as a term of art because to do so deprives the language of a fine word in its original connotation. If gay means homosexual, we can no longer sing *Our Hearts Were Young and Gay* or *A Bachelor Gay Am I* without being misunderstood.

But there comes a time when the most obdurate linguistic purist has to bow to the dictates of usage, and there can no longer be any doubt that the word has been accepted as common currency and is here to stay.

It is one thing to accept the term, it is another to accept the fact. Or so it would seem from the coyness with which the obituaries in the Australian press tiptoed around the sexual preferences of Sir Robert Helpmann.

There can hardly be anybody in Australia with a most casual interest in the arts or, indeed, anybody among the general public whose knowledge of public figures extends beyond a few sports people who did not know that Helpmann was homosexual. And he made no attempt to conceal it himself.

In England, homosexuality in high places has long been accepted as a fact of life hardly more worthy of notice than a person's preference in cars. Yet in the *Times* of 29 September came an obituary of Helpmann which was considered by some to be a bit below the belt.

The questionable sentence was this: 'A homosexual of the proselytising kind, he could turn young men on the borderline his way.'

If one accepts as I do the right of men and women to choose their sexual preferences, why should a homosexual man not pursue male partners as a heterosexual man pursues female partners?

As for young men on the borderline, that is a position on the sexual spectrum which almost invariably culminates in, at the very least, homosexual experimentation, regardless of whether there is a Svengali-like figure, as Helpmann is here pictured, hovering around ready to pounce.

It has long been acknowledged that fame is an aphrodisiac and renowned men with heterosexual preferences have always taken advantage of their *réclame* to persuade women, often much younger than themselves, to jump into bed with them. In fact, such sexual triumphs are widely applauded and regarded as one of the deserved fringe benefits of male achievers. Surely it is a form of sexism to deny similar privileges to men whose sexual preference is for other men.

The *Times* is now a Murdoch-owned newspaper. Murdoch has acknowledged that he intervenes in the running of his widely scattered media outlets. His presence hovers like a conservative Big Brother over the pens of his journalists throughout the world.

Is it too far-fetched to suggest that the writer of Helpmann's obituary in the *Times*, sensitive to what he guesses are his master's prejudices, and yet conscious of the British tolerance of homosexuality, felt that he might earn a few brownie points by smearing Helpmann with a hint of pederasty?

One imagines Helpmann was hardly the sort of achiever who would have been an idol to a man like Murdoch. But in England it would have been out of character for a quality newspaper to suggest that there is anything odd about a famous man being a homosexual. Even Murdoch may have heard of Proust, Forster, Cheever, Cocteau and of some eminent Australian homosexuals.

In short, the *Times* obituary may be regarded as a Murdochian variation on the general British theme of sexual tolerance.

While we are on the subject, it is high time that the Australian media became less sexually prissy. Another example of their conservatism in the reporting of matters with a sexual connotation is their inhibitions in the use of commonly used words for sexual intercourse.

There is something schoolmarmish about the blank spaces

in f . . k. In all but the most genteel circles that is a word that is accepted as the most direct and lucid term for what it describes.

Admittedly you would not expect the word spelt out in a Murdoch paper, even though such a paper would regularly seek to boost its sales by displaying on a prominent page a pair of t . ts spilling out of a bra. But I suggest that the *Sydney Morning Herald*, as Australia's leading quality newspaper, set an example by spelling the taboo word in full.

Karl Marx was fond of quoting the maxim 'Nihil Humanum A Me Alienum' ('Nothing human is foreign to me'). Although I would never suggest the *Herald* take on a Marxist tinge, it could do worse than to adopt that precept.

16 October 1988

GREAT, FLAWED CHARACTER

I knew Lionel Murphy warts and all, and there were plenty of warts. I deplore the rather sickening hagiography which threatens to canonise him and bury the real man in the process. The essential Lionel Murphy can stand scrutiny and still emerge as the great, flawed character that he was. Who needs saints anyway?

One man does, Mr B. A. Santamaria. Writing in the *Australian* this week, he depicts Murphy as a satanic figure, the central purpose of whose life was 'to remove, if not extirpate, the moral and social values of Christianity'.

The basis of this allegation is a statement by the historian Manning Clark on ABC television on the night of Murphy's death: 'I see Lionel Murphy as a man who . . . strove to end the domination by God over human beings, by one class over another, by a parent over a child, or by a man over a woman, or by a husband over a wife.'

Murphy would have gladly accepted that definition of his guiding philosophy. He was an unabashed atheist and a debunker of what he considered outworn shibboleths.

Manning Clark's estimate of Murphy's motivation was based on his belief, grounded on his personal knowledge of the man, that 'he believed passionately that the morality of Judeo-Christianity has ceased to be relevant'.

It is at this point that the self-righteousness of Santamaria and his kind asserts itself. There are plenty of people, I among them, who have rejected the notion of God without necessarily concluding that everything in the Judeo-Christian ethic is dispensable.

Nothing annoys me more than the smug imputations of the Santamarias of this world that you can't be good if you don't believe in God. On the contrary, a good case can be made out for the superior morality of the person who strives to lead a good life without fear of punishment or hope of reward.

I would hazard a guess that Santamaria never met Murphy. If he had had the slightest personal acquaintance with him, he would have known that the Judeo-Christian virtues of compassion and turning the other cheek were exemplified in him.

He was a man who inevitably stirred up enmities, but I never heard him speak a word of personal denigration of his harshest critics, even during the travail of his last two years. I envied him his charity which, I confess, I do not share.

But the real casuistry of Santamaria's assessment of Murphy emerges in his attribution to him of a philosophy of nihilism, of not believing in anything.

Once again he relies on some statements of Manning Clark which have nothing to do with Murphy. In his eulogy of Murphy the historian stated, according to Santamaria, that 'the con-temporary world has lost faith, not only in God but in the Enlightenment as well'.

On another recent occasion, Manning Clark lamented that the present generation was 'probably the first generation which doesn't believe in anything at all'.

Then Santamaria reaches the startlingly illogical conclusion that, on the strength of Manning Clark's general observations, Murphy can be adjudged to have been a supporter of 'the far more tyrannical domination of the nihilist "new class" which rules society today'.

In the first place, Murphy did not belong to the generation of which Manning Clark was speaking. In the second place, anyone who knew Murphy more than superficially realised that he was almost naively an optimistic son of the Enlightenment of 'Voltaire, Rousseau, Diderot and all that', to adopt Santamaria's contemptuous dismissal of those great figures.

One of the most endearing – or, from a nihilist point of view, infuriating – of Murphy's qualities was his belief that there was a rational cure for most of society's problems. I don't suppose I have ever met anybody who was further from being a nihilist.

A closer reading of Santamaria's article discloses that his real grievance against Murphy is the latter's role as a sexual libertarian and, in particular, his piloting through the Parliament of the Family Law Act.

At this point the voice of our Savanarola rises to a strident pitch: 'It was meant to extirpate the institution of permanent monogamist marriage and replace it with a purely temporary contract, once known as concubinage.'

This is mind-boggling rubbish. Which is the more humane approach to the eternal problem that a certain percentage of marriages inevitably break down: to insist that, in the absence of some fault such as desertion, violence or infidelity, the marriage is indissoluble; or to face the reality that the continuation of such a marriage is bad for the parties and even worse for the children?

Murphy's other offences, in Santamaria's eyes, include 'passing human rights acts, sexual discrimination acts and equal opportunity acts'.

History will put both Murphy and Santamaria in their places. Both have played a prominent public role in recent decades, but I venture to suggest that the ultimate verdict on each of them

will have little to do with their services or disservices to God
or to Judeo-Christianity.

6 November 1986

ORDERING HUMAN AFFAIRS AT THE MARKET

The celebration – or lamentation, depending on your point of
view – which attended the tenth anniversary of the reign of
Margaret Thatcher raises interesting questions about the future
of capitalism and socialism.

Her admirers regard her achievement as having proved that,
by dismantling a government-supported economy, she has
shown that small government is better than large government,
producing the result that in the past two years Britain has
emerged as the fastest-growing economy in Europe. The yuppie
generation which her policies have spawned has deified her for
having put paid to the question: does capitalism work? But the
answer is not as simple as they claim.

Thatcher is a radical conservative. As Margaret Jones pointed
out in her comprehensive review of a spate of recently published
books, both pro- and anti-Thatcher, she saw her first task as
being 'to smash the power of the Conservative Old Guard and
to replace the grandees with her own men of the New Right'.

Perhaps her obvious admiration for Gorbachev is based on
his success, so far, in a similar crusade in his own country: to
root out the political and bureaucratic fossils of a stagnant
economy as a prelude to making it work. And like most adherents
of her political and economic philosophy, she would undoubtedly view Gorbachev as the harbinger of the death of socialism.

Like most practising politicians whose horizon is limited to
the next election, she would be too busy attending to pressing
daily tasks to find time to contemplate the larger question: does

the 'death of socialism' guarantee the survival of capitalism?

A more philosophical thinker, the distinguished American economist Robert Heilbroner, has confronted this question in a temperate and scholarly article in a recent issue of *The New Yorker*. He asserts, without any of the gloating which characterises the more simplistic worshippers of capitalism that, fewer than seventy-five years after it officially began, the contest between capitalism and socialism is over: capitalism has won.

But his conclusion is sobering for the market idolators:

I do not think that the triumph of capitalism means its assured long and happy life, or that the defeat of socialism means its ignominious exit from history. The collapse of centralised planning shows that at this moment socialism has no plausible economic framework, but the word has always meant more than a system of economic organisation.

At its core it has always stood for a commitment to social goals that have seemed incompatible with, or at least unattainable under capitalism – above all, the moral, not just the material elevation of humankind. However battered that conception may be from the designation of bloody and cruel regimes as "socialist", the vision has retained its inspirational potential, just as that of Christianity has survived countless autos-da-fé and vicious persecutions.

I suppose it may be said that whether or not it is now intellectually disreputable to describe yourself as a socialist depends on your definition of the term. At least for Western socialists, except purblind Stalinists, it never involved approval of one-party tyrannies. And Gorbachev has now implicitly confessed that such a political straitjacket has unsustainable economic costs.

Political scientists and economists used to speak of the possibility of a historic convergence of the two systems but such a vision has long been out of fashion. Heilbroner suggests:

Perhaps the vision will again become a matter for serious consideration if the extraordinarily difficult movement of centralised socialism toward economic and political liberation is not derailed, and if the drift of

capitalism toward a more responsible amalgam of economic freedom
and political responsibility continues its slow historical advance.

The proponents of 'pure' capitalism – which, of course, has never existed any more than 'pure' socialism – see as their ideal the exclusion, as far as possible, of government from carrying on or regulating or otherwise becoming involved in the workings of the market system. It is this philosophy which inspires drives for deregulation and privatisation.

The main contest in Western democracies has centred on what is the appropriate line of demarcation between the roles of government and of business.

Contrary to the hopes of those who read the Soviet retreat from a rigorously planned economy as vindication of the need for a diminishing role for governments in the ordering of human affairs, Heilbroner points out that the tendency in all capitalist countries has been and will continue to be toward an enlargement of the role of governments in the management of their economies.

He points out that one of the forces promoting such an enlargement of the political realm is 'the increasing power of industrial technology to puncture the protective mantle of the environment – a development that has moved all governments to intervene in the productive process to safeguard the human habitat against disturbances caused by industrial processes and products'.

It is interesting to note that the high priestess of smaller government, Margaret Thatcher, has recently moved to the forefront of the worldwide movement for governments to face the threat to the ecosystem posed by the greenhouse effect.

Those who read Dr Edward Linacre's lucid exposition of the subject in the *Herald* of 9 May will realise that the greenhouse effect amounts to nature presenting its bill for man's excessive use of the world's resources. That sacred cow, the free play of market forces, has nothing to offer as a solution to the problem it has created. It is, as Linacre points out, a global problem calling for a global solution.

It is not just a matter of a few scientists getting their heads together and providing a quick technological fix. It is a matter for governments and it involves such matters as limitation of populations, more modest standards of living and the equalisation of nations. In Linacre's words: 'The problem is a symptom of how far we are from having a sustainable economy.'

Those who see a diminishing role for governments as the desirable and historically progressive way to go are whistling in the dark. Another thing Marx was wrong about was that the State would ultimately wither away.

14 May 1989

SOME PRAISE FOR MALCOLM – THROUGH GRITTED TEETH

King's Hall is the agora – 'marketplace' – of the Federal Parliament House. Members have to pass through it on their way to work, it is a natural place for their exchange of gossip and it is where the visiting public can gape at the over-publicised politicians who have been transformed by the media from nonentities into celebrities.

If you keep your eyes peeled in King's Hall, you can often gain a clue to the 'treasons, stratagems and spoils' being hatched in the corridors of power.

The last months of 1974 and the early months of 1975 were turbulent times in Canberra. Snedden's hold on his party was slipping and nobody was doing more to make him lose his grip than Malcolm Fraser, who had always believed that he had been sent by God to lead the conservatives and the country.

One night about this time, I was crossing King's Hall on my way to my office. A famous old journalist – one of the characters of the place, deeply conservative, racist and sexist, a bit of a joke to the new wave of media men and women just then making their appearance in Canberra, but nonetheless regarded with some affection as a dated curiosity – pulled me up and said rather boozily: 'Cop that for a scene, Jim.'

He pointed to two men in deep and earnest conversation in a far corner of King's Hall. They were Malcolm Fraser and Neville Bonner.

After I had focussed on the pair, the old journo remarked: 'Look at Malcolm chatting up that little black for his vote. If he strayed on to Nareen, Malcolm would sool the dogs on to him.'

I could not dispute this assessment. Visions of the early pastoralists chasing the Aborigines off their ancestral lands, shooting them down if they gave any trouble, and finally subjugating them and using them as menial hands, sprang to mind.

Malcolm Fraser – to my mind the archetype of the Bunyip aristocrat, haughty and sure that he was born to rule – would obviously harbour one of the basic prejudices of his kind, contempt for black people.

After he became Prime Minister, he emerged to almost everybody's surprise as an anti-colonialist champion of the rights of blacks to self-determination. I was unable, in the light of my estimate of Fraser's character, to take this stance seriously.

I have had occasion to observe that men with the egotistic drive necessary to endure all the pain and boredom involved in becoming Australia's Prime Minister soon discover, after winning the prize, that they don't amount to a row of beans on the world stage. You can almost hear them asking: is that all there is?

Ineluctably, they begin to aspire to a global role. This was what led Menzies to make such a fool of himself before the United Nations General Assembly over Suez, where Nehru cut him down to size before the eyes of the world.

None of our Prime Ministers has been able to resist the temptation to cut a dash in the big world beyond our shores. Billy Hughes made a noisy contribution to the disastrous peace settlement after World War I, which guaranteed that there would be World War II.

His disgraceful performance and the odium which it subsequently earned him did not deter his successors from trying their hands at world statesmanship. At the last CHOGM, Bob Hawke made his own characteristic ocker contribution to this hallowed tradition.

When Hawke nominated Malcolm Fraser as Australia's Eminent Person in the group charged with persuading Botha and company that they should gracefully bow out of business rather than hang around until their throats were cut, I protested on two grounds: first, that it was a fruitless exercise; and second, that it was obscene for a Labor Government to do anything to reinstate the reputation of the man whom I regarded as being as blameworthy as Kerr in the events of November 1975.

My view that the EPG exercise was a futility has been confirmed by Fraser himself. As he wrote in this paper (16 June): 'It is clear that gentle diplomacy and quiet persuasion have failed. We believe firmly that the South African Government will never be moved by such approaches; that it will, in fact, be moved only by pressures; and that what it has done so far, little as it is, it has done as a result of international pressure.'

Fraser is smart enough to have known all that in advance. But although I do not resile from anything I have said about the uselessness of CHOGM or the setting up of the Eminent Persons Group which it fathered, I must confess to having developed doubts about my assessment of the character of Malcolm Fraser.

Reading closely what he has said about the cataclysm which appears almost certain to engulf South Africa, I am persuaded that he is motivated by a sincere anti-racist philosophy.

It is possible that this attitude may be based as much on pragmatic as on humanitarian considerations. In warning the countries with the greatest economic stakes in South Africa, especially Britain, he is at pains to point out that if history is to take the inexorable course which will flow from the Afrikaaner ascendancy's policy of suppression of black aspirations, British investors will sooner or later have to write off their holdings in that country.

By imposing sanctions on South Africa, British stake-holders will be short-term losers, but if they don't do something (and sanctions are the only effective option), they will finish up losing everything.

The direst possible result for any country with a large financial stake in another country is that the latter should become a communist State.

The Americans, especially, have constantly justified their support for some of the most blood-drenched dictators on the grounds that, although they may not have liked a certain régime, it alone could prevent a Marxist takeover.

Up to the last moment, the Americans propped up the corrupt Batista regime in Cuba. They lost all and got Castro. In the Philippines, Marcos was their man and they were lucky that he was not supplanted – as his replacement Aquino may still be – by a communist régime.

Fraser's message to Thatcher and Reagan is: do you want another Castro in Pretoria? He turns out to be a more sophisticated defender of British and US interests in South Africa than Thatcher or Reagan.

The Fraser recipe may save something from the wreck for the British and US bankers. Trying to prop up the defenders of apartheid is, as Fraser points out, a bankrupt course which will ensure that all is ultimately lost.

It must be apparent by now that it sticks in my craw to give any applause to Malcolm Fraser. But whatever his philosophical motivation, I am unreservedly on his side in his campaign to persuade the only people who may be able – by the imposition of the sternest sanctions (namely Thatcher and Reagan) – to lean on Botha and company to go far enough, and that will be a long way, to satisfy black aspirations and prevent a bloodbath.

I do not share the view, which I have heard expressed in recent times, that Fraser may be about to take advantage of the present disarray in the Liberal Party to make a comeback as its leader and ultimately as Prime Minister.

His present role as leader of world public opinion in the fight against apartheid would, I believe, strike him as more important than being the leader of a country which is largely unnoticed by the rest of the world.

And he would be right.

19 July 1986

55

IS BRILLIANCE ENOUGH?

Now that Paul Keating has been touched by the hand of God, having been anointed by the Prime Minister as the man most deserving to succeed him, it is worth our while to examine seriously his credentials for the top job.

I well remember one day in about 1980 when I was walking down Queen Street in Sydney's Woollahra, and I happened to glance into Bill Bradshaw's antique shop and caught a glimpse of Paul chatting to the proprietor.

He beckoned me inside and the three of us were soon in animated conversation about the merits of Empire clocks, about which I knew nothing. It did not take long to realise that Paul had already made himself an expert on the subject.

As I live nearby, he drove me home and stayed awhile. When he left, my wife, who had never met him before, remarked: 'That's the most brilliant politician I have met.'

I agreed with her then and I still hold the same opinion of him. But is brilliance enough or is it even the most important ingredient in a political leader?

Hawke, whatever you may think of him (and I have repeatedly made it clear that he has no place in my political pantheon), has to be recognised as one of the most saleable Prime Ministers in our history. His record of three successive electoral victories speaks for itself. He obviously has what the people *think* they want.

The point is that he has got there without the faintest glimmer of brilliance. (The ranks of Rhodes Scholars, incidentally, contain plenty of mediocrities.) He is an unoriginal thinker, a soporific speaker and he has been spared any touch of wit. Probably the only Prime Ministers we have had who would qualify as brilliant are Bob Menzies and Gough Whitlam.

When I arrived in Canberra, Paul was already there and, despite the large gap in our ages, we soon became friends. It was not because we were philosophical soulmates but each of us found the other entertaining and we provided each other with some comic relief from the *longueurs* of that mostly boring place.

I have seen almost nothing of him since that day in Queen Street but I have watched his career with a mixture of admiration and misgiving. I fear that his fatal flaw may turn out to be his facile capacity to acquire almost immediate expertise in anything to which he turns his mind.

Unwittingly, he gave a clue to the shortcomings of such facility when he engaged recently in an exercise in promotion of his image of himself as a cultivated man by giving a little sermon on Jeffersonism and Neo-classicism.

Neo-classicism, far from being a revolt against the past, as Keating suggests, was, as the very name suggests, based on a return to the standards of ancient art, especially the art of Greece and Rome. What it had to do with Jefferson is far from clear.

He succeeded in demonstrating that his self-acquired erudition in the field of the arts and history is as narrowly based as in the field of economics and that the shallowness of his learning does not entitle him to the certitudes that he pronounces and to the contempt he expresses for those who do not share them.

Speaking of the Neo-classic style he is reported to have said: 'You couldn't get any better. They hadn't been any better since, and, since deco, there have been only fag packets and bottletops.'

No, Paul, the tone which you adjudge to befit your attacks on Wilson Tuckey is not appropriate to your campaign to sell yourself as a Renaissance man. In the field of art, dogmatism and exclusiveness are marks of the limitations, not the breadth, of your learning. To brand as rubbish everything which does not appeal to you may be the mode in knockabout parliamentary debate but not when you are wearing your connoisseur's hat.

In short, the capacity to do a crash course in Neo-classical art does not confer on you the right to speak, artistically, ex cathedra.

The capacity to absorb the Treasury's view of economic reality and to master its jargon does not entitle anybody to ridicule any dissenting views of the *humane* way to deal with our troubles. The omniscient former Treasury guru, Senator John Stone, has surely cast some doubt on the infallibility of Treasury by placing himself at the service of an economic primitive like Bjelke-Petersen.

Keating is overreacting from the sloppiness of Labor's traditional thinking on economic matters, especially on the part of its now-defunct Left. Is it unscientific, maudlin 'politics of the warm inner glow' (a favourite pejorative expression which Keating has purloined from me) to be appalled by the phenomenon of homelessness in Australia and to advocate doing something about it, even in our present straitened circumstances? Is compassion (that wimpish word) inconsistent with good economic management?

I suggest that the very narrowness of Keating's economic expertise, based solely on the advice of the currently fashionable value-free breed of positivist economists precludes that scepticism and open-mindedness which are the hallmarks of the authentic cultivated human being.

Has it ever occurred to him to have a glance at models other than those beloved of the orthodox economic pundits?

I have nothing but admiration for his acquisition, on the basis of very inadequate formal schooling, of skills in the field of economics and the arts, but crash courses are no substitute for genuine erudition, which provides the best inoculation against the illusion that you – or anyone else – know all the answers and that your critics can be written off as sentimental fossils. It will be a pity if such a gifted human being cannot match character with intellect. His performance to date leaves a big question mark over his capacity to be anything more than clever. And that's not enough. If I were a betting man I would have a little flutter that Paul is more likely to finish up among the multi-millionaires whom he so admires than as Labor Prime Minister.

10 September 1987

P.S. Nothing illustrates the perils of political prediction more than the last sentence. As other pieces on the subject of Keating indicate, I have vacillated and am still vacillating on his likely future.

On the Road to
The Damascus Rainforest

A politically innocent friend asked me recently: 'What is a numbers man?' Not being in a mood for exegesis, I replied: 'Graham Richardson.'

I concede that that was a cop-out but Richardson, in his own person, is the complete answer.

That still leaves the question: What is Richardson?

Ideologically, he is a totally empty man.

Overnight, he became a born-again Greenie when a survey conducted in 1986 by Labor's pollster, Rod Cameron, indicated that Labor's apparent indifference to conservationist issues was alienating a growing section of the community to whom such issues were more important than anything else.

Up until then, I doubt whether Richardson would have known a melaleuca from a marigold (he probably still doesn't).

He then proceeded to convert Bob Hawke, until then a man who was uncomfortable unless he could feel the bitumen under his shoes, but who is now, at least pictorially and at election time, a nature-lover.

That's one of the functions of the numbers man: to know, as the Americans put it, what will and what won't play in Peoria, or in other words, are there any votes in it?

The moment Richardson became convinced that there were votes in conservation was his moment of truth on the road to the Damascus rainforest.

I noticed the other day that he described himself also as a theatre-lover.

I am among Sydney's inveterate frequenters of the theatre and I must confess that I have never seen his cultured countenance at a play.

That, of course, will change now that he has been awarded the portfolio of Environment and the Arts.

Richardson is a man to whom politics is about nothing except winning, and that is the role of the numbers man: to see that his side wins.

His side is not just the Labor Party, but the right-wing Mafia which has controlled the NSW branch of the ALP for as long as I can remember, which is the dominant force in the Federal Parliamentary Labor Party, and which put the once slightly leftish Hawke where he is today.

The Labor Party has changed a great deal since I was a member of the Federal Parliament, but one thing has remained constant: factionalism.

What often goes unrecognised is that the party has never been a monolithic structure; rather it is a coalition of forces ranging from starry-eyed nationalisers of everything to people whose attitudes on social issues are just slightly to the left of Fred Nile.

What also has been given insufficient attention is that the membership of a faction can often be as much a matter of preselection as of ideology.

If you live in an electorate where the majority of the members of the branches are Lefties, and you want to get into Parliament, it doesn't take much perspicacity to work out that it pays to be a Leftie – and vice versa.

Richardson, from the outset, pinned his colours to the right-wing mast in NSW because he could see that was the surest way up.

But in addition to the gift of being value-free, he needed something more to emerge from the ruck and become an influential figure in the Labor Party.

What were the qualities which made him the leading numbers man and ultimately won him the prize of a portfolio against so much more talented opposition?

The role of the numbers man is to whip people into shape,

to make sure that they toe the factional line and are not so deflected by arguments of principle or conscience or personalities, as to allow their votes to stray from what is expected of them by those who control or can affect their political fate.

A numbers man develops an uncanny gift for being able to pick the defector in a secret ballot whose aberrant vote may have made the difference between victory and defeat. He or she is then marked down for retribution.

I have experienced this in my own person, though to expatiate upon the example would be too tedious. But this is just the point. The numbers man must have an innate capacity for tedious detail.

He is constantly on the phone or engaging in face-to-face persuasion, twisting arms, promising advantage, threatening disadvantage, counselling against quixotism, enforcing conformism.

It is a sleazy, boring, inglorious role, but to a certain type of individual it is the meat and drink of politics. Richardson is the paradigm of the species.

There still remains a mystery about Richardson. Charisma, or charm, or intellect, are among the words one would not apply to him.

How has he managed to exert such influence, indeed to inspire so much fear?

This is the X-factor in politics, as in many spheres of human endeavour.

The appearance of having power can actually confer power.

Richardson emerged from a NSW machine where he earned a formidable reputation as a factional manipulator.

The word gets around that, for aspiring or practising politicians, it is good to have certain people on side, and unwise to have them as enemies.

People who are basically nonentities get the reputation of being king-makers or political assassins.

The tireless, undistinguished mole burrowing away day in, day out, can and does play an important role in deciding the fates of people who are his moral and intellectual superiors.

They also employ a system of IOUs: 'Now listen, mate, it may stick in your craw to vote for the Australia Card, but there's a trip to the States coming up this year.'

When Richardson presented his own IOU to Hawke for his key role in undermining Bill Hayden's grip on the leadership in 1982, thus opening the door for Hawke, the latter was obviously not game to resist his demands.

Hawke proved subsequently that he could get his way when he insisted on more women and more Queenslanders being in his Ministry.

If the Prime Minister had said 'over my dead body' to the project to dump that excellent performer Barry Cohen, in order to give Richardson his job, he could probably have pulled that one off too.

But he judged that it would be unwise to refuse to cash Richardson's IOU.

However, all is not lost. Every now and then, there is a win for the adage: 'Those who live by the sword shall perish by the sword.'

19 February 1987

Money Maniacs

Pity our poor tycoons. Consider what can happen to just one of them in the space of a couple of weeks. Wouldn't everybody understand we were just jesting if you or I had, at a party after the conclusion of the Olympic Games when the Foster's was flowing, grabbed a member of the Olympic planning body by the tie and told him that, if he didn't vote for gentlemanly Melbourne (where, after all, Foster's is brewed) in preference to loutish Sydney as the venue for the next Olympic Games, we'd set the dogs on him?

But when the news broke that John Elliott had suggested that the exercise of such a preference would provoke him into organising a financial boycott of the Games by Australia's biggest corporations, he got treated as some sort of a business thug.

How could anybody get such an impression from the most cursory examination of his record? After all, he is prime ministerial material.

Why can't people appreciate the sacrifices to which our tycoons submit in order to help make Australia great? His totally disinterested, non-paying job as president of the Liberal Party involves Elliott in physical endurance tests beyond the capacity of anybody but a superman.

To attend the recent executive meeting of that party, he had to travel from Melbourne to Canberra by his own executive jet after reportedly sitting up all night on a flight from London, where he'd been busy trying to take over another brewery. These jets, I am told, are fitted out like luxury apartments, so I wondered why he didn't take a nap. Evidently, tycoons are too busy slaving for their country to find time for sleep.

But the greatest indignity of all is the way he and his kind are persecuted by that ogre, the Taxation Commissioner, Mr Trevor Boucher, who has picked out a hit-list of major corporations for a special tax audit.

Last year, the Tax Office squeezed an extra $100 million out of such audits and is threatening another $60 million by next July.

In the interests of those industrious, self-sacrificing fellow tycoons who are being scrutinised in this high-handed example of bureaucratic effrontery, John Elliott felt propelled to accuse the Tax Office of being anti-business and posing a threat to the democratic system.

But what gratitude did he get for such devotion to the commonweal? One editorial in a reputable paper had the gall to point out that, if the Tax Office fails to collect what is due from the big boys, then a greater tax burden falls on the mugs from whom it is taken at the source by the PAYE system.

I'm a bit old-fashioned about these things, and I've often wondered, as does Mr Boucher, how tax avoiders can bring themselves to use the roads, schools, hospitals, parks and other

63

vital amenities and services for which they expect others to pay.

Switching off Elliott, who must be this country's greatest incitement to violent revolution, let's take a look a poor embattled Bondy. Fancing having to divert his energies from such patriotic endeavours as the takeover of Tiny Rowland's Lonrho in order to defend himself before the Australian Broadcasting Tribunal for having paid $400 000 to another great patriot, Sir Joh Bjelke-Petersen. (By the way, why don't we hear any comments on the morality of Sir Joh's accepting the money, or, as some might put it, soliciting it?)

In short, there appears to be little public gratitude for the efforts of the entrepreneurs, who are merely trying to make Australia great. It's that tall poppy syndrome again.

If I may desist from the diversion of jesting about sacred things (like money and the Olympic Games), allow me to confess that I have never been able to penetrate the psyche of the tycoon. As the old song in the movie has it: 'What's it all about, Alfie?'

They live lives of self-inflicted jet-lag and face the contumely of all but a small circle of sycophants and fellow megalomaniacs. They mostly eschew the pleasures of social relaxation, aesthetic indulgence and travel for enjoyment rather than business. They endure the constant perils of living by the sword.

In the small hours of the nights when they are at home, or during the sleepless watches over the Atlantic or Pacific, do they ever pause to reflect: Holmes à Court, once worth (on paper) more than $1 billion is now probably down to his last $100 million, Laurie Connell will probably soon be down to his last string of racehorses, could it be my turn next?

To be sure, the danger that you may ultimately be down to your last $100 million is not all that dire. Perhaps it is the loss of face involved in being demoted from number one or number two to number 200 on the dollar honours list which bothers them most.

But why not get out when you've got that $100 million? Surely the only explanation can be that the accumulation of wealth and the power that goes with it are addictions not all that dissimilar to alcoholism.

If the alcoholic is a person who dares not take one drink

because he can't stop when he's had a half-a-dozen or so but must keep going until he passes out, the money maniac is just as incapable of stopping at $100 million, and must keep going, regardless of the danger of passing out financially.

Well, for a healthy, well-endowed human being with a range of choices in a world of manifold avenues for self-expression, tycoonery doesn't strike me as much of a life. It is, of course, preferable to the lot of the millions of victims who seem to grow more numerous as the wealth of the few increases.

But I repeat, this time seriously, my opening words: Pity our poor tycoons.

23 November 1988

THE EDIFICE COMPLEX

Junkies, so I am told, get a *frisson* of pleasure from even handling a hypodermic needle. For politicians and the powerful, pleasure comes from an even less likely source: the foundation stone.

The desire among such people to express themselves in bricks and mortar – or pre-stressed concrete and mirror glass – amounts almost to a neurosis; an edifice complex, in fact. The phrase is not mine, but no other describes more aptly the state of mind which regards a building not as a structure but as a self-glorifying assertion.

Take the most recent example: the announcement of not one but three separate towers, to be built in Queensland, each of which is to be bigger than Sydney's Centrepoint Tower. Building the biggest is very important to those with an edifice complex. I need not dwell on the symbolism involved. Bigger than Centrepoint! Golly!

Or take the new Federal Parliament House. It was not always a foregone conclusion that Capital Hill, where it is now rising inexorably, would be the chosen site. An argument raged for years between the protagonists of Capital Hill and of Camp Hill. The latter is little more than a gently sloping mound just behind the existing Parliament House. It was argued that by encroaching on this mound with a building to house the services which were overloading the present Parliament House, the useful life of that building could be extended for many years.

In the new building would be located the Hansard people, the catering services, the ministerial advisers and hangers-on, and the media. Thus, even with an expanded Parliament, the low-level building where, after all, much of what passes for our history has occurred, could continue as the locale for the familiar political drama (or farce, according to your point of view). That was the plan which appealed to me.

Every time the Senate ran out of business somebody would suggest putting the question of the site for the new Parliament House on the notice paper. The parties agreed that it would be a free, non-party decision. In the final debate I advanced the Camp Hill option. I was eloquently supported by John Button.

But we were steamrollered by the edifice complexes of all parties. Their view was encapsulated in the words of one senator (whom I paraphrase from memory): 'The bureaucrats are down here [on the Canberra plain]. We who govern the country should be up there [pointing to Capital Hill] looking down on them.' It was some time before the preposterousness of such a statement was revealed by *Yes, Minister*.

That was the edifice complex as a manifestation of collective megalomania. More frequently the malady is individual. Although he did not design the High Court Building on the southern shore of Lake Burley Griffin, that clinical specimen of the edifice complex, Sir Garfield Barwick, could not restrain himself from taking a hand in its detail, so compounding the aesthetic disaster which it was doomed to become in any case.

Another individual manifestation of the malady is the building in Paris which houses our present Ambassador to UNESCO, who describes it as the *Palais Seidler*. The Australian Embassy, an animal whose bloodlines may be traced back to Gropius and Le Corbusier, is really a riposte rather than a building. It is not every day that an architect, especially an Australian, gets an opportunity to thumb his nose at the traditional glories of Parisian architecture by designing his version of a good building right in the heart of Paris. Harry Seidler certainly grabbed his chance to indulge his quirky edifice complex.

While we are on individuals we cannot overlook our own Neville Wran. His fixation on the 'beautification' of Darling Harbour may have its origin in his boyhood. To a sensitive lad commuting between Balmain and the City, this area would have been one from which, after a while, he would instinctively have averted his gaze. Some day, he may have said to himself, 'When I am the Pericles of Sydney, I will erase this eyesore and build an edifice by which I will be remembered'.

I don't suggest that a casino or a monorail had a place in his musings. Life had to mould him somewhat before such prosaic possibilities were superimposed on his dream. (By the way, Neville deserves full marks for what may well turn out to be his most lasting and praiseworthy edifice: the Wharf Theatrical Complex at Walsh Bay. It is as good as anything of its kind in the world and not at all vainglorious.)

Some cities have the edifice complex, some don't. Sydney, despite the Opera House, does not. The Opera House did not result from some great surge of civic aspiration. When that wily old philistine, Joe Cahill, announced, almost as an afterthought towards the tail-end of an election campaign, that he could let us have an Opera House for, as I recall, some £3 million, the reaction of the man in the street was: 'Well, I'll cop that so long as it doesn't cost any more.' The Opera House did not become a subject of general interest until the cost estimate blew out to the shock-horror (but today peanuts) figure of $100 million.

Sydney takes itself for granted. It smugly believes that it is so beautiful that it needs no make-up.

Not so Melbourne. That attractive city is built on a flat, featureless plain, bisected by an insignificant muddy river. From the start it needed all the help it could get.

Its inhabitants took up the challenge to such effect that Melbourne, from a man-made point of view, has long outclassed

Sydney, which without its waterways and undulations of terrain would be a commonplace city. Melbourne's streets are wider and leafier, its gardens more lush and extensive, its domestic architecture incomparably superior to Sydney's. (Sometimes I think that the people who designed the early houses of Sydney and Melbourne never visited the other city. There is no cross-fertilisation between the two).

And, like the plain sister of a beautiful woman, Melbourne has constantly striven to make the most of herself. When a Sydney person visits Melbourne, some local patriot is likely to point to the tasteful adaptation of an old building into a modern hotel and the question is left hanging in the air: 'Do you think you could do that up there?'

Yet despite its achievements, Melbourne is still in the grip of the edifice complex. The city hankers after some monolith which will say 'Melbourne!' to all the world. It has had competitions to entice designers to plan such a thing. So far, thank God, they have not produced much – but give it time.

The Melbourne-Sydney thing has become the subject of so many jokes as to have become a cliché. It contains nonetheless the truth which is embedded in every cliché. Melbourne's edifice complex owes much to its communal inferiority complex.

But that, after all, does not really matter. As the Jewish woman who was told by a psychiatrist that her son had an Oedipus complex replied, 'Oedipus Schmoedipus! So long as the boy loves his mother!'.

6 February 1986

A BIG APPLE WITH A ROTTEN CORE

'The great big city's a wondrous toy, just made for a girl and a boy . . .' and, with due respect to the songwriter, for a mature woman and even for a reasonably active geriatric.

On a recent visit to New York, as on my periodic forays into the Big Apple over the past thirty years, I spent the first few days in almost yokel-like awe of the sumptuous spread laid before me.

But I must confess that, as both the city and I have aged, neither of us for the better, I have become increasingly aware of the meanness, even cruelty, which tarnishes its magnificence, even though my infatuation has not been totally extinguished.

The centre of the imperial city is more glitzy than ever. At least one new tower is under construction on almost every block, disrupting the already tangled traffic by the inevitable intrusions of the construction process.

Some of the additions since I was there in 1977 are, even by New York's standards, staggeringly grandiose monuments to opulence, such as the Trump Tower on the corner of Fifth Avenue and 57th Street (forty-one-year-old Donald Trump is Bond, Packer and Murdoch rolled into one).

The splendid museums which house the art looted from the Old World, expiatively bequeathed to the city by America's billionaire conquistadors, are still thronged mostly by ordinary men and women from everywhere.

Great theatre, especially that distinctively American invention, the musical, still flourishes. You don't have to be rich (though it helps) to enjoy a lot of the entertainment on offer.

For US$4 each, my wife and I enjoyed a great musical treat at the Lincoln Centre. It was a dress rehearsal for a concert to be given that night in the same place to commemorate the seventieth birthday of a New York icon, Leonard Bernstein.

The NY Philharmonic Orchestra, accompanied by male, female and boys' choirs (there must have been 200 performers on stage) performed a couple of early Bernstein works under the direction of Zubin Mehta.

The large hall was full. Sitting next to us was an elderly, blind music lover who had made the journey alone from Greenwich Village to Columbus Circle to hear the music.

And there are manifold other delights: lunch in Central Park, strolling along the thronged historic streets of the Lower East Side, whose very names – Mott, Mulberry, Orchard, Delancey,

Lafayette – recall all the fables you have heard of the poor immigrants who sought refuge from the miseries of the Old World and some of whose children became millionaires.

This time I enjoyed the new experience of walking across Brooklyn Bridge to explore the architectural delights of Brooklyn Heights, an area of elegant brownstones looking across the East River to the Manhattan skyline – for my money the most delectable residential area of New York.

But unless you avert your gaze from all that does not please the eye, you cannot help noticing the disfigurements of this marvellous city.

Walking through Columbus Circle after an evening show at the Lincoln Centre, you are confronted suddenly by the sight of human bodies huddled on makeshift pavement beds under the awnings of a marbled tower. The homeless, mostly blacks, are settling in for the night as the theatregoers make their way to their comfortable apartments. Oh, Calcutta!

The homeless also sleep in the subways and the grand railway terminals, although there are periodic attempts to turf them out on to the streets. It has been estimated that on any given night 50,000 people doss down in the subway.

New Yorkers are not unkind. But they have become inured to human misery through the sheer frequency of their contact with it. It is as much a part of the daily round as the sun rising in the east and setting in the west. They rarely make eye contact with the outcasts.

A committee set up by the National Academy of Sciences – a high-powered private organisation which advises the government on policy issues in the field of science and health – has just issued a report which had been requested by Congress. The academy prides itself on its apolitical, value-free objectivity. The composition of this particular committee reads like a who's who of the American academic establishment.

It cited a 1988 report estimating that 735,000 Americans are homeless on any given night while 1.3 million to 2 million will be homeless for one night or more in a year. It seems likely that these figures are greatly underestimated.

Ten of the thirteen experts on the panel took the extraordinary step for such a conservative body of issuing a special supplementary statement to express their 'anger and dismay' at the extent of the social tragedy disclosed by their investigations. The language of their supplementary statement has a Dickensian resonance in recording the human degradation and despair of the homeless.

So was homelessness a big issue in the presidential campaign? Let's look first at the man who won – George Bush. He has been described by one commentator as 'a fellow for whom any question – even one so simple as "what day is this?" – is a trip wire'. He is not a bad man, but like the previous incumbent, he doesn't seem to have much idea of what is happening in the real world.

He is famous for his gaffes, as when he said: 'I hope I stand for anti-bigotry, anti-Semitism, anti-racism.'

In the non-events which were called the Presidential Debates when the question of homelessness came up, Bush repeated the 'thousand points of light' phrase he has constantly used despite its opacity. It evidently is intended to mean that homelessness could be solved by charity work.

Dukakis was slightly more positive but still vague. It is an issue which is easily outranked by so-called value issues like patriotism, abortion and 'liberalism', which may be summed up as the crime of believing American society is less than perfect.

Another regular contribution to NY life is made by the crazies. They stand on the sidewalk, ranting and gibbering or merely muttering quietly to themselves. They are almost totally ignored by the passers-by. America has a new class of invisible men and women.

Occasionally their mental disturbances take on a more active aspect, as in the case of the man who stripped naked opposite St Patrick's Cathedral in a fashionable section of Fifth Avenue, rushed into the church and clubbed a seventy-six-year-old usher to death before being shot dead by a police officer.

Most of the city is dirty and untended, with bags of garbage piled up on the pavements.

If it were not for the almost superhuman skill of NY drivers, especially cab and bus drivers, the traffic would hardly move.

In the daily accounts in the media of the doings of the mega-rich, the Calcutta-like chasm between those at the top and those at the bottom is made manifest. The ugly face of greed is nowhere better exemplified than in the case of the Helmsleys. Leona (69) and Harry Helmsley (79) are on charges of evading taxes of about $4 million by charging construction work on their upstate mansion to their hotel and real estate empire. What is a puny $4 million to a couple worth $5 billion?

A good start in changing America's big cities from being a precarious amalgam of glittering, high-tech palaces and of Third World squalor, would be to get a philosopher-king into the White House.

But there is no philosopher-king (or queen) on a horizon where the transition at the top is from the Gipper to the Gaffer. Both of those characters are fond of invoking the eye-moistening prayer, God Bless America. Perhaps it should be God Help America.

1 November 1988

IF I RULED SYDNEY

I had a dream recently that Barrie Unsworth had done a Louis Napoleon and appointed me his Baron Haussmann.

When he summoned me to his office, I was much impressed by his erudition. 'You remember what the baron did for Paris?' he said. 'When old Louis made him prefect of the Seine back in 1853 he told him to rip the guts out of the CBD. That's how we got the Champs Elysees and a lot of beaut new buildings. Now that we've got rid of Laurie [Brereton – a former minister for works] I want you to clean up the mess that he and those before him have left us. As I've said before, I see Sydney as the

Paris of the Pacific. Also I've got an important occasion coming up [an impending election] and I need some runs on the board.'

'But Premier,' I demurred, 'the Haussmann caper cost Louis a lot of money and got him into serious political trouble.'

'I know,' replied Barrie, 'but I've got those urban greenies baying at my heels and we've got to get back to basics. As far as money is concerned, Bob's your uncle.'

I decided to start at the southern end of the Central Business District. The first and most obvious eyesore screaming for demolition was the NSW Institute of Technology on Broadway. This vast, concrete, Stalinesque prison was obviously designed to damp down the demand for tertiary education.

But once you have conquered that deterrent and penetrated inside the dungeon, you are inclined to bury your head in your books because the windows are so placed that you have to stand on a table to view the sweeping vistas of your city. In any event, you can't see through the windows before the overhanging eaves prevent the use of the usual window-cleaning mobile scaffolding. Down with that one.

While we're in the area we might as well slip around the corner into Jones Street and take a good look at the Fairfax building. I don't remember which of these two horrors came first. One obviously inspired the other. I put my pencil through that one too, emboldened by the thought that Barrie would see that the simplest way to end the Fairfax Conspiracy was to deprive them of a building.

Then around the corner to Darling Harbour. Apart from the ugliness of that big hangar the Exhibition Building, and other individual structures, the whole scheme is misconceived. I have always believed, together with Neville Gruzman, that the appropriate development of this area should have been a new inner city suburb of low-income houses with supporting amenities, surrounding a bicentennial park.

The more people we have living in or near the city the more animated it will become. And what a boon a lung, a smaller version of magnificent Centennial Park, would be on the western fringe of the city. The pencil went through the whole lot, with the exception of the Chinese Garden, which could be incorporated as a harmonious feature of my park. I almost forgot to mention the monorail but there are no prizes for guessing what I did to that one.

I soon realised that to do justice to my brief I would have to recommend the demolition of everything in the CBD any higher than the AWA Tower which, when I first arrived in Sydney after the war, dominated the skyline from the harbour.

But the worst scars on the once-lovely face of Sydney are located in the Quay area. Down with the Cahill Expressway, for starters. I demolished Harry Seidler's Grosvenor Building and would make him rebuild the old Johnson Building at his own expense.

That awful row of mediocre buildings along the east side of the Quay which block the view of the Opera House from the south would go, leaving a handsome forecourt to our most beautiful modern building. It is too early to pass judgment on the covered walkway still under construction so I left it out of my interim report.

All plans for the Gateway Building I recommended for the rubbish bin. The Regent Hotel survived my pencil but I'd knock down the old facade of the Shipp Inn. It was an ugly pub when it was functioning and now what's left of it is even uglier. Age alone should be no guarantee of a building's right to survive.

In putting the pencil through the two AMP Towers, I lamented the fact that our ancestors had missed out on an opportunity to build our own Champs Elysees, starting at the Quay, embracing Macquarie Street and Hyde Park and continuing as far as Central Railway. But I baulked at recommending that because I knew I could never convince Barrie to move Old Vic again, especially now that she's got Bert the Good gazing fondly at her from the other side of Macquarie Street.

Finally to Sydney's heart, Martin Place. The Mall was a wonderful idea but why allow it to be defaced by the messy MLC Centre or the glitzy, pretentious glass house, the State Bank? Down with both of them and out with all the excrescences which interrupt the view of the Mall from Macquarie to George Streets.

And, of course, the very, very first to go – that macho, phallic Centrepoint Tower. The destruction of that assertive erection would symbolise the termination of what developers have done to Sydney, if you take my meaning.

The task Barrie had set me did not take me long on the demolition side. As to what should fill all the resultant holes in the ground I decided that could wait until I'd given him my interim report. When I gave it to him with the sketch I'd made with all the gaps in it he said: 'Bewdy, mate, this will solve the unemployment problem as well.'

I asked him if he had any preferences for filling the holes. He brushed me aside. 'Don't you worry about that,' he said, keeping alive a dying tradition. 'I'll get an artist to draw some pretty replacements for the vanished buildings and show them on every TV screen. After we win the election, you can take the model home and put it on your patio. We won't be needing it any more.'

3 December 1987

B LARNEY,
EVEN WITHOUT KISSING THE STONE

Malcolm Fraser would love *The Irish Times*. When first elected Prime Minister he promised to make politics so uneventful and crisis-free that there would be no news for the front page, which would thenceforth be devoted to sport. While *The Irish Times* has not quite succeeded in putting sport on the front page, it has achieved the next best thing: five pages of sport following the page one news.

The trouble about visiting Ireland is that its tear-jerking songwriters, both resident and expatriate, have turned a lot of it into a bit of cliché.

Perhaps it was because of this that on our recent visit, my wife and I did not bother to depart from our chosen itinerary in order to include Tralee, whose rose named Mary had the truth in her eyes ever shining; or Tipperary, to which it is a long way to go to look up the sweetest girl I know; or even the Blarney Stone, traditionally a must for politicians.

But such is the embarrassment of riches with which Ireland is endowed (scenically, not economically) that you could miss almost every place which has featured in a song and still gorge yourself on its beauty.

We landed at Shannon airport and drove at a leisurely pace up the western coast. Having been warned that it rained almost every day in Ireland, we were surprised to strike six days of sunshine out of seven, even though it was raining in other parts of Ireland where we did not happen to be.

When I told this to a barmaid, she remarked in all seriousness: 'The good Lord is smiling on you. You must be living a very holy life.' Saintliness is easily earned in Ireland.

While there is an abundance of lush greenery, especially in the south, to our eyes the most spectacular landscapes were the stark bare hills of the promontories and their hinterland along the Atlantic coastline: Connemara, where we came across Ireland's only fiord, which goes by the name Killary Harbour and which ends up at a little town called Leenane, sleeping in timeless indifference to the world beyond its hills; and Donegal, from the town itself where the world's best tweed cloth is made, to the bleak north-western tip of the island.

There's a trap up there for the unsuspecting tourist. It is predominantly Gaelic-speaking, and the signposts, in this worst-signposted of all countries, are in that language, while the names on your map are mostly in English. While The Bride, who was driving, always purported to be on top of the problem, there were times when I feared we might make it into the media as missing persons.

It takes a while to realise that, scenically, surprise is the norm. At one moment you are passing through picture-postcard greenery with sleek, handsome cattle and blackfaced sheep (so laid-back that they settle down for a rest on the curves of the narrow roads and cast the onus on drivers to get around them) and with an occasional ruined abbey or castle. Almost all ruins are attributed to Cromwell.

Then, abruptly, you are surrounded by peat bogs, and the next moment the hills rise and you are gazing at what could be the face of the moon.

This unpredictability rubbed off on our own behaviour. At one moment, as reverent Yeats-lovers, we were gazing at the great man's tomb in the graveyard of St Columba's (Protestant) Church, a few kilometres north of Sligo.

A couple of hours later we were in a slightly less dignified situation when The Bride got herself locked in a lavatory in a murky pub where we stopped in the hope of lunch at a little fishing village called Killybegs on the north coast of Donegal Bay.

In retrospect, though not at the time, it was a hilarious experience. But as a popular song has also conferred cliché status on such a calamity, I will refrain from digressing. Suffice to say that she was able to climb through the narrow space between the loo partition and the ceiling and to reach safety via a ladder held by the giggling staff, who found much fun in her plight. The proprietress commented: 'You're a solid woman but luckily, not too solid.'

The 'troubles' of Ireland – the atrocities of the unceasing civil war between the IRA and the British Government – had been far from our thoughts as we savoured the beauty through which we passed. But having spent as much time as we could afford in the west and the north of the Republic, our trip south involved a short passage through Ulster. Reality hit us when we proffered Irish pounds to pay for petrol in the ugly town of Enniskillen and the garage attendant muttered (somewhat disparagingly): 'Irish money.' He had a thick Irish brogue.

At the border, as seems inevitable in this laughing yet lugubrious country, gloom was diluted by the comic. We were stopped at a checkpoint and our passports were inspected. After satisfying himself that we were not terrorists, the fresh-faced twenty-year-old English soldier said: 'Australian, eh? Do you come from Melbourne?' Why was he interested in Melbourne? 'That's where they make "Neighbours".'

He was a constant devotee of that soapie, though he didn't think much of Kylie. Foster's (available in every Irish pub we visited) and 'Neighbours' have put us on the map.

The Ring of Kerry, Killarney and a town called Clonmel, which is a surprising amalgam of ancient Irish charm and sophisticated modernity, are our outstanding recollections of the south. As garden-lovers we made the obligatory trip to Powerscourt, one of the world's great gardens, in the Wicklow foothills a few kilometres south of Dublin. It's as good as its reputation.

Why are there only five million people in this beautiful but largely empty country? Simply because you can't eat charm and beauty. For various reasons, including the deliberate policy of the English overlords who ruled it for centuries, the Industrial Revolution largely passed Ireland by.

But in a land where contraception has always been a sin against God and large families an inevitable result, this backward country, though most of it is incredibly fertile, has never been able to match the fertility of the Irish. That's why Ireland's greatest export has been Irish people. And there are more of them in Boston, New York, Liverpool, Sydney and Melbourne than in Ireland itself.

But the spin-off from Irish economic backwardness has been the preservation of the charm which might have been engulfed by 'progress'. In the parts through which we journeyed, there were no roadside advertising hoardings, few freeways separating wayfarers from the surrounding landscape and very few cars to overtax the narrow roads.

A few of the larger cities showed the scars of modernity. As we entered Galway, where there has been some European Community investment, we passed through a characterless area typical of the outer suburbs of any industrial centre. It was the only place where we saw a McDonald's. I began to fear the fabled old city had been swallowed up by the developers, as have so many of the world's great settlements, including our own. But I am happy to report that old Galway is still there and still a sight for sore eyes.

We averted our gaze as we passed through the dreary outskirts of Cork and Limerick and even that great navigator, The Bride, was fully stretched (and very cranky) in seeking sufficient guidance from the enigmatic signposting to get through those famous but now unlovely cities.

The task of getting through Dublin was so formidable that we had only a cursory look at its Georgian elegance and did not even have time to explore the Martello Tower from which 'stately plump Buck Mulligan' emerged on the first page of Joyce's *Ulysses*.

We left Ireland wondering whether backwardness is the price to be paid for the preservation of loveliness.

10 November 1988

MIXED BLESSING FOR THE MOUNTAINS

'What the Japanese did for the Blue Mountains in the 1940s is nothing to what they are going to do in the 1980s,' a Mountains real estate man remarked to me recently.

This wryly cynical comment recalls the exodus of some of our privileged citizenry from their harbourside haciendas after Japan's mini-submarines penetrated the waters of Port Jackson, which had not known an invasion since 1788. The preferred havens for many of these patriotic fugitives were the sylvan fastnesses of Leura, Blackheath and Wentworth Falls.

And now that tourism has become one of the lifelines of our beleaguered economy, it is not surprising that the exceptional scenic attractions of the mountains are looming larger in the itineraries of the most determined and affluent tourists of the Pacific area.

The Japanese presence in the mountains is becoming more patent, but only as part of the general upsurge in visitors to the region. I have never seen more people in the area than during a recent holiday weekend.

What has been a relatively depressed area for years is facing a renaissance. Depending on the way you look at things, its future is full of promise or menace.

There is going to be a lot of controversy about the Blue Mountains in the years ahead. Extreme, dogmatic positions will be taken, there will be plenty of pontificating and, consequently, plenty of need for calm, dispassionate thought. And since fashion decrees that no subject is worth discussing today except in economic terms, our starting point presumably should be that the Blue Mountains are to be considered a precious resource.

No matter how hard-headed your approach, it surely makes sense that the silliest way to exploit a precious resource is to destroy it in the process of exploiting it. The Blue Mountains will take some destroying, but man's proficiency in that process should never be underestimated.

The best book on the area that I have read is one published in 1985 by the Macleay Museum of the University of Sydney, called *The Blue Mountains: Grand adventure for all*. It is a series of essays by an assortment of authoritative experts. One of them, Julie Stockton, gives us the best and simplest starting point with her opening line: 'The Blue Mountains have a fresh-air economy.'

She cites a passage from travel writer Frank Hurley's 1952 book on the area: 'In one major direction the various towns on the Blue Mountains are unique. They possess no industries, either primary or secondary. They grow nothing and they make nothing . . . They subsist entirely on the tourists who come to view their scenic splendours and breathe their pure air.'

Tourism got a fillip as the sustaining industry of the mountains during the gold rushes of the 1850s. As fortune-hunters made their way west to the goldfields, they stopped at inns on the way, spending money. Gradually the attractions of the mountains themselves, the scenery and the fresh air, lured a sufficient flow of day-trippers and holiday-makers to support a permanent service industry.

There has always been a leavening of affluent people who can afford large houses in which to live, either permanently or occasionally, in the mountains. In addition, artists, who find they can paint or write just as well – or better – in the mountains as in a large city, have always had a presence there.

The metropolitan housing crisis has further increased the population of the mountains, since houses are much cheaper there than in the city.

This, of course, involves the nuisance of daily commuting for mountain dwellers whose work is in the city, but that is preferable to not having a roof over your head. In any event, thousands of city-dwellers also are condemned to much tedious commuting from the suburbs of the ever-more-sprawling city.

But what my real estate commentator had in mind was a vast expansion of the economy of the Blue Mountains, based on massive investment in upmarket tourist facilities in the area. For him, the way forward is illustrated by the Fairmont resort constructed near the northern tip of the Leura Golf Course, on the edge of the Jamison Valley escarpment, with sweeping vistas towards Mount Solitary.

As one who had reservations about it in the first place, I have to concede that it is a tasteful development, blending a traditional mountain and oriental-style of architecture and that, when fully landscaped, it will cause minimal damage to the natural environment.

There is some Japanese capital in the enterprise and, since it offers first-class accommodation, it is already on the Japanese tourist circuit.

Will there be more Fairmonts in the Blue Mountains? Is it, as the more fervent of the greenies fear, the thin edge of the wedge for the vulgar Gold Coasting of this beautiful area?

The future of the Blue Mountains is delicately poised. Environmentalists often are depicted, by those to whom development is nigh unto godliness, as narks who seek to deny to others the beauties which they enjoy themselves. The tourist industry has worked up a big head of steam in this country and the greenie lobby is being pushed onto the defence. It would be rash to believe that the rape of the environment is a peculiarly Queensland or Tasmanian phenomenon.

It is a situation which will call for vigilance and sensitivity on the part of all decision-making bodies concerned with the future development of the mountains. From a purely materialist point of view, it should be borne in mind that our treasures must be preserved if the world is to be cajoled into paying to see them.

22 June 1988

YOU PAYS YER MONEY, AND YA GETS YER CHOICE

The almost universal pleasure with which the news was greeted that something bothersome had happened to Alan Bond tends to confirm the suspicion that our media tycoons are not among our most popular citizens.

Whatever ensues from the adverse findings of the Australian Broadcasting Tribunal, Bond's difficulties should be placed in the perspective of the changing times for television proprietors generally.

The days when a broadcasting empire was worth $1 billion (and it's open to question whether one ever was, although that's what Bond paid for Kerry Packer's Channel 9 interests) will soon be gone forever. A new ballgame is coming up in which a television licence will no longer be a licence to print money, and the industry will become much more competitive.

There is a deep irony in the fact that the foremost advocates of deregulation in our society are themselves about to become the victims of deregulation in their own industry.

Of course, the deregulation which has been all the rage among TV licensees has been the elimination, or at least minimisation, of program regulation. One form of regulation which is dear to their hearts, and central to the profits which have hitherto accrued to the possession of a licence, is the existing limitation on the number of commercial television channels.

Enter the villain of the piece: pay-television, which will

provide the first real, commercial (that is, not ABC or SBS) competition for existing commercial television since the third commercial licence was granted in Sydney and Melbourne in the 1960s.

What is pay-television? Essentially, it means that consumers pay to receive, with special equipment, a television signal. These new television services will provide additional and different programs from those available at the moment. The new channels may show, for example, news only, sport only, first-release movies, or arts and cultural programs, thus appealing to special interests among its audience ('narrowcasting') rather than aiming for the greatest proportion of the audience at all times (broadcasting).

Pay-television is about expanding viewer choices, at a price, of course. But we Australians have shown ourselves eager to try new technology; look at how we jumped at video recorders and fax machines, and these are not cheap. There seems little doubt that many of us will be prepared to pay to see something different or of special interest to us. And there is little doubt that pay-television will come. The biggest questions are when and how. At the moment there is a moratorium on its introduction until 1990, but there is enough activity on the pay-television front to suggest that existing licensees will not be able to hold the line much beyond that.

In April 1988, the then Minister for Communications, Gareth Evans, initiated a departmental review of policy options for the introduction of pay-television. In February this year, a report emerged from this inquiry. The issue is also being examined by the House of Representatives' Standing Committee on Transport, Communications and Infrastructure.

Predictably, in their submissions to the inquiry, commercial television interests urged that pay-television not be introduced until 1992-93 at the earliest and that it should not carry advertising.

Leaving aside this special pleading, there are certainly questions of importance to be considererd before the Government gives the go-ahead. The biggest is how pay-television will be distributed, as this will affect the number of services available and the number of viewers able to receive them.

If pay-television is distributed by cable, as many as 60 channels may be available. Who needs 60 channels? You may well ask; in the US where there are many cable channels available, research shows that most people never watch more than about half-a-dozen. Cable pay-television would almost certainly mean a heavy involvement by Telecom in the distribution system, which may strike terror in the hearts of anyone who has ever done battle with that monolith.

If pay-television were to be distributed by satellite (which means we'd need dish antennas at home), fewer pay-television channels would be available. Some may think this is not such a bad thing.

Whatever mode of distribution is used, pay-television adds up to a big headache for existing commercial licensees, allowing plenty of room for the play of the market forces theoretically so dear to the hearts of those who wallow in the advantages of their monopoly.

It will be ironical if – as seems almost certain – it falls to the lot of a Labor Government to introduce pay-television. After all, Labor can scarcely be said to have trimmed the sails of the media moguls. Moreover, the ALP's much-trumpeted cross-media ownership rules have been seriously threatened by a recent Federal Court decision which seems to allow virtually unlimited time for proprietors to dispose of assets which breach the rules.

And the introduction of pay-television would place the government under enormous pressure from existing licensees to relax controls on program matter – such as those which require them to screen Australian programs – as a trade-off for deregulating the number of channels. The Australian Broadcasting Tribunal, which administers these controls, may well be in the hot seat again (a position to which it must be becoming increasingly accustomed). We must hope it continues to show the same independence and toughness it manifested in the Bond decision.

14 April 1989

WHATEVER ELSE IS
FAULTY THE LEAK SYSTEM WORKS

Love will find a way, and so will an enterprising journalist. When the new Parliament House was unveiled to the gaze of those who will have to pay for it, fears were expressed that its impersonal vastness, so different from the endearing slummy unprivacy of the old one, would make it more difficult for the press gallery to pry and to keep attuned to the scuttlebutt which is grist to its mill.

The segregation of our lawmakers from the hoi polloi, including the media, is in stark contrast to the inescapable intimacies of the old King's Hall and the corridors so narrow that two people going in opposite directions could hardly avoid physical contact.

The new place is to the old place like Vaucluse or Toorak to Newtown or Fitzroy. But it is already obvious that it takes more than a change of habitat to alter the mores of pollies and journos.

The minute details of the recent skirmish between the Prime Minister and the Treasurer which were served up to us by old hands like Alan Ramsey, Paul Kelly, Mike Steketee and Laurie Oakes gave notice that despite the elevation of the Parliament from the plain to the mountain, the press gallery will not be disadvantaged in its pursuit of the trivial as well as the profound.

A leak is still a leak and fly-on-the-wall reports of what happens in face-to-face private encounters between our statesmen will still be as forthcoming as before.

This is in the nature of the political process. There has not been a great number of politicians who have been able to earn or maintain respect of many discerning journalists. But no matter what they think of each other, they need each other.

The symbiotic relationship which develops between them is

based on journalists' constant need for news and politicians' hunger for the sort of publicity that will reassure those who put them there that they made the right choice.

Members of the press gallery get from their contacts (leaks) a self-serving version of what is happening behind the scenes. Those who are worth their salt soon learn how to sift a grain of truth from a tonne of self-promotion.

Much has been written about leaks, and every now and then some politician who has been offended by the disclosure of matters he would have preferred not to see the light of day remonstrates about the disloyalty of leakers. This occasional lapse into a high moral tone rarely deters the complainants from leaking what they believe might be to their advantage.

Members of the parliamentary élite who have made it into the ministry don't need to soil their hands on such chores as leaking. They leave that to their staff, who, of course, have been briefed by their ministers on what to leak and how to slant it.

I'm told that Henry Kissinger was so vain that when he was Secretary of State he insisted on doing his own leaking, as he didn't trust anybody but himself to give the exact nuance to his strategies for managing the world in the interests of American hegemony. The sophisticated political reader soon learned to replace the words 'authoritative source' with 'Henry Kissinger'.

Here, the straight-from-the-horse's-mouth type of leak tended, in the time before the present teetotal, jogging ministry, to come from the mouths of bibulous ministers in the non-members' bar.

During my brief sojourn in the sanctum of the sages, even before I made it into the ministry, I was on the information gathering list of the more diligent members of the press gallery.

I remember an occasion when there was a changing of the guard on one of our major newspapers and a journalist with whom I was known to be on close terms was replaced by one I hardly knew.

One day after a Caucus meeting I returned to the monastic cell which passed for an office in the old building to find my friend's replacement already ensconced there, pen poised.

I was a little terse with him for taking so much for granted. Politicians who are willing to grant the favour of their lucubrations to earnest seekers after knowledge still like to think they deserve a little courtship before being prepared to disgorge their secrets.

Genuine friendships can exist between journalists and politicians but the politician always has that same lingering doubt which must haunt the rich woman about whether she is being courted for her sweet self or for her money.

In an article in a recent issue of the *Bulletin*, my old and present friend Barry Cohen, while acknowledging his continuing addiction to parliamentary gossip, entered a mild lament that 'vital national issues are analysed more in terms of how they affect the future of individuals than the impact on the future of Australia'.

If it were possible for high seriousness to be the exclusive tone of politics and political reporting, he would, of course, be right. But it isn't, and I'm afraid we have to settle for some infusion of the cult of personality even in our more responsible political reporting.

If our quality press is to continue to have readers, some concession has to be made to the public's appetite for news about gladiatorial contests between individuals as well as the issues around which their contests are fought.

The general standard of political reporting, which in our quality press compares favourably with that of overseas papers, is not diminished by dishing up a bit of entertainment between the serious stuff, so long as it is not overdone.

Speaking for myself, I must confess that I find a political mini-series like the Hawke–Keating punch-up almost as gripping as the Fitzgerald Inquiry.

And if you have lived in Canberra, as Barry and I have, you would have to admit that if it weren't for the occasional outbreak of egomaniacal buffoonery, the political milieu would become quite intolerably boring, especially for the press gallery.

When politicians complain of media beat-ups they are not

taking the ground of high political seriousness but admitting that they don't like what the media are saying about them. They have no objection to a favourable beat-up.

12 September 1988

Can Bob Find True Love at Last?

In the light of the Federal Court's interpretation of the Broadcasting Act it would be interesting to know if the Prime Minister took any legal advice before giving his blessing to Rupert Murdoch's plan to take over the Herald and Weekly Times.

Hawke's threadbare justification for his passive support of Murdoch's takeover betrays his shallow approach to the principle involved.

He is reported to have stated that it would be impossible for Murdoch to do the government more harm than had the 'viciously anti-Labor' Melbourne *Herald*.

While justifying a hands-off attitude in the interests of the operation of market forces he believed that the Trade Practices Commission's scrutiny of the carve-up of the HWT interests, and the government's announced policy on cross-media ownership, would provide sufficient protection for the public interest.

It does not matter to the public whether Murdoch turns out to be more or less anti-Labor than the Melbourne *Herald* has been. What does matter is that, even after he has divested himself of the lesser newspapers which might bring him into conflict with the Trade Practices Act, Murdoch will still have about twice as much print space as the *Herald* and its kindred publications had, distributed all over the country, in which to be pro or anti whatever he chooses.

It is not just that it is Murdoch, although as I will explain, I have the least regard for him. John Fairfax and Sons, the publishers of the *Sydney Morning Herald*, yesterday announced a takeover bid for the Herald and Weekly Times. I would be just as opposed to Fairfax – or Holmes à Court, or Bond – owning 60 per cent of Australia's print media.

It is too early to be precise about what newspapers Murdoch may finish up with, especially in the light of the Federal Court's decision, which puts the whole deal in doubt. But if it stands up legally the probable outcome will be this: because of his deal with Holmes à Court his presence will be least obvious in Perth, although he will still probably own one paper there.

In South Australia he will have the only morning daily, the *Advertiser*. In Victoria he will have the mass circulation morning tabloid, the *Sun-News Pictorial*, the afternoon broadsheet, the *Herald*, several magazines and 11 suburban newspapers. In NSW he will have the morning tabloid the *Daily Telegraph*, the mass circulation *Sunday Telegraph*, the *Australian* (also circulating in other capital cities), the afternoon tabloid the *Daily Mirror*, four Sydney suburban newspapers and 22 regional newspapers.

In Queensland he will have the leading Brisbane daily, the *Courier Mail*, the afternoon *Telegraph* and the *Sunday Mail* (the existing Murdoch papers, the *Daily Sun* and the *Sunday Sun* will be sold). He will also dominate the Queensland regional market.

In Tasmania he will own the *Mercury*, a daily, and the *Sunday Tasmanian*. In the Northern Territory he will own them all. He already owns ten South Pacific publications.

Hawke is, as he has been throughout Murdoch's raid, silent on what amount of concentration of print media ownership is contrary to the public interest.

Does Hawke have a view on this subject? Is sixty per cent, the amount which is expected to remain under Murdoch's control after divestiture, too much? If so, will Hawke be briefing counsel to urge the Trade Practices Commission to compel further divestiture? His attitude up to now suggests to the contrary.

My view is that he fears above all the consequences of offending Murdoch and that he has given him assurance that he will do nothing to impede his empire-building. And that, I believe, from any Prime Minister and especially from one claiming to be Labor, amounts to an abandonment of responsibility to the people of Australia.

To their shame, the politicians of all parties have abstained from the debate about this great issue. (Did Murdoch time his coup to coincide with the period of the great annual Australian torpor, when many of our politicians are recuperating from the rigours of office in the world's pleasure spots, and the general public has just completely turned off?) The discussion has been conducted almost entirely in the media and in a slightly hysterical atmosphere. (Will we all finally end up working for Murdoch, or will we be garbos?)

When Malcolm Fraser, once the exemplar of Australian conservatism, but lately way to the left of Hawke on most issues, weighed in with a suggestion that legislation should be introduced limiting the ownership of print media by one proprietor to thirty per cent of total daily circulation, the alarm bells started to ring for the anti-government interventionists.

Peter Robinson (*Australian Financial Review*, January 20) warned that that would take us along the South African path. The over-riding principle was 'simply that of anyone's right to create and print a newspaper', subject only to laws designed to prevent criminal slander.

'For my part,' he stated, 'if I had to choose between more competition from the Murdochs and Holmes à Courts of this world and more interference from the Duffys, Frasers and Macphees, I'd choose Murdoch any time.'

With due respect to Peter Robinson, and at the risk of being lumped in with his 'trendy harpies', those comments miss the point as much as Hawke has missed it.

It is a long time since Adam Smith and nobody suggests any longer that we should all be allowed to drive on the right side of the road if we want to. It is possible to adhere to Hawke's faith in 'a free enterprise economy which is based on the operation of market forces' without anathematising all government controls.

Peter Robinson concedes the need for the application of some government controls of the electronic media, but only for technical reasons: 'The airwaves are ultimately a finite resource and have to be allocated in some rational way.'

But control of the electronic media is not limited by technical considerations. What technical consideration is involved in the prohibition on a foreigner owning more than fifteen per cent of a TV station? Surely another, un-technical value consideration has been imported into our TV laws, namely the undesirability of control of such an important means of communication by a person whose allegiance is not to this country.

Why should this consideration not also apply to the print media? I would always be loath to resort to a xenophobic or jingoistic argument, especially as it is usually the last resort of most opponents of everything I believe in. But surely there is a rational justification, based on the national interests, for preserving control of all of our media in Australian hands. Imagine the public reaction if a Soviet citizen or a representative of Yasser Arafat were to make a takeover bid for an Australian newspaper chain.

Rupert Murdoch has renounced his Australian citizenship and sworn allegiance to the US. I have no doubt that when he talks to Hawke he proclaims himself to be still an Australian at heart, but there is little evidence that heart plays much of a role in his daily transactions. He is in law, and in his primary interests, an American. Despite the arithmetic (to employ one of his favourite terms) of his recent Australian activities, his American media activities loomed large enough in his considerations to induce him to abandon his Australian citizenship.

We can confidently expect from his Australian newspapers – if his takeover stands up legally – an uncritically, pro-American line. Even though Australia is an ally of the US, I for one do not believe that our interests always coincide. There are, of course, American newspapers which provide highly critical comment about official American policy, but Murdoch's track-form does not suggest we would get much of that from him. He is a thick-and-thin Reagan supporter and a natural barracker for the Establishment.

Finally, I must freely confess an interest: I have a great distaste for Murdoch, for his cynical modus operandi and for his shoddy newspapers. He is a great debaser of every publication he gets his hands on. That witty, far from leftie Englishman, Auberon Waugh, has described him in the *Spectator* this month as a 'hairy-heeled, tit-and-bum merchant'. The more Murdoch papers we have the lower will be the quality of Australian journalism.

As to Hawke's expectations of what cuddling up to Murdoch will do to further the only real interest which he has – to be the first Labor leader to win three Federal elections – I would remind him of a warning which I have already given on a previous occasion: when Labor jumps into bed with big business it would do well not to mistake a one-night stand for eternal love.

22 January 1987

IS JOHN LAWS NECESSARY?

I suppose every big city has its John Laws. He is an inescapable fact of modern life.

Two preconditions must exist for such a figure to emerge. First, the likelihood that during certain hours of the day a large proportion of the population with access to a radio will be so occupied as to seek some not-too-demanding aural diversion.

Ready examples are drivers; housewives engaged in various chores which engage them physically but not mentally; people in institutions such as hospitals; and shift workers. The essence of their condition, at least for the time being, is loneliness and radio offers the simplest way out of their isolation.

It is obvious that on any day a big city like Sydney or Melbourne will provide such a large captive audience.

Second, a person with a gift for communication. Obviously, there is a lot of competition for such an audience. In Sydney, serious talk and music are available without the interruption of commercials from the ABC and MBS and not-so-serious talk and music from a variety of commercial stations. To get on top of the competition and stay there a radio personality has to have something. And Laws has it.

What he has is marketability. That is, he has what a lot of ordinary people want or can be talked into wanting. These chronically or temporarily lonely people want somebody to talk to and listen to who is more or less on their own level, but whom they can be persuaded to regard as a bit above them, somebody they can look up to.

It is reasonable to assume that people of demanding tastes will choose one or other of the alternatives to Laws when they find themselves in need of passive radio diversion. I have heard some of them express anger and surprise at what they got when switching across his wave-length. He is not the intelligentsia's cup of tea.

He doesn't need to be and he knows it. To be an ordinary bloke, one of the mob, is part of his stock in trade. But he has to be a bit more than that. The only exceptional gift of this basically commonplace man is a fine, clear voice with which he manages to give a resonance to shallow opinions that convinces his listeners out there that their mate John is also a bit of a guru.

By this trick he manages to persuade a lot of people that the trivial pub/cab chit-chat which comes as naturally to him as to them has a little touch, but not too much, of profundity. He also has the knack of making the thoughts of others appear to be his own. One day when I listened to him he was pontificating on the follies of John Valder. I also had read the morning papers. His remarks seemed merely a paraphrase of the editorial comments of that morning. Perhaps he is convinced that a lot of his listeners don't read the papers.

True, he suffers from certain shortcomings. Sometimes he finds it hard to suppress his impatience at having to listen to voices other than his own. His grip on the language is somewhat tenuous. The other day he had great delight in demonstrating his erudition to a woman who phoned in to compliment him on his choice of words and to ask him the meaning of a word he had used, 'apropos'.

He told her, correctly, and for good measure threw in a little homily on the common error of using the word 'of' after the word. But in the same program he used the non-word 'vetinarian' and in another program I heard him disclaiming guilt for something for which he had been 'castegised'. But his greatest device for authenticating his status as a bit of a personage is his obvious intimacy with and ready access to leading public figures. Since every politician knows that Laws has a large audience they fall over themselves to get on to his program. An invitation to appear on his program is almost a command.

Neville Wran is apparently available to speak to his friend John at the drop of a hat. It is instructive to observe the subtle changes in Laws's demeanour towards his political interviewees, ranging from deferential to patronising to bullying, to contemptuous. It's like the difference between the salutes which are given to a field-marshal, a general, a colonel and a lieutenant.

With Wran he is respectful but buddy-buddy. He is more like the champ's sparring partner in the gym than the serious fighter who is out to hurt him in the ring. He never lays a glove on the Premier, who always emerges looking as though he'd just stepped out of the shower.

Neville Wran deserves full marks for being able to arrange for himself such a service from Australia's leading media salesman. The unspoken trade-off between these two public figures is immediately obvious. In return for providing Wran with a guaranteed large audience, Laws is rewarded by Wran's genuine or simulated regard for Laws's sagacity and concern for the welfare of the common man and woman. (I loved Laws's compassion when speaking as a gentleman farmer to a rural battler making $6000 a year.)

When Paul Keating was on Laws's program recently they chatted like a couple of Woollahra gentlemen whose real interests were far from vulgar materialism and gouging in the clinches. Paul launched into his clever act of simplifying the complexities of our economic problems with John sitting back self-effacingly and performing the radio equivalent of nodding sagely in agreement.

John is an authority on most subjects, but, like the rest of us, he is a bit out of his depth on economics. In the same week that he interviewed Wran, he also interviewed George Paciullo, who is a long way down the pecking order of public figures. George, Minister of Police in Wran's Government, adopted an attitude to Laws which could perhaps be described as grovelling. Laws, in turn, treated him like some little poodle he was teaching to perform tricks.

There are some people who regard Laws as some sort of menace to society. That, I believe, is taking him far too seriously. There are more sinister influences on politics and politicians than John Laws, but they are mostly inaudible and hence less irritating. The worst that can be said about him is that the accoutrements of a mere huckster do not equip him for the role of political analyst and commentator to which he evidently aspires. Laurie Oakes or Max Walsh he is not. But after all, nobody is compelled to listen to him.

1 April 1986

TACKLING SUPERPOWER POLITICS

Nobody dies harder than a cold-warrior. We have a clinical specimen in the egregious Alan Jones, broadcaster, columnist, star of the celebrity speaker circuit and formerly esteemed rugby coach.

He has devoted his regular column in the past two issues of the *Sun-Herald* to admonishing those whom he sees as gullible fools for taking Gorbachev at face value and believing he is a genuine advocate of détente.

Among those dupes who can't see through the deceit which Jones believes to be as much a part of a Russian leader as his party card are Margaret Thatcher and our sacred Queen. Jones's splenetic outbursts were provoked by the reception Gorbachev got from those two ladies on his recent triumphal visit to England. It is almost as though the once super-Anglophile Alan had developed an anti-London complex.

Reagan, of course, who was finally induced by the performance of Gorbachev to retract his evil empire anathema, and the venerable George Kennan, former adviser to American presidents and the inventor of the policy of containment, who spoke up recently in praise of the Gorbachev-led thaw in East–West relations, would also qualify for our self-appointed Sovietologist's strictures.

The basis of the Jones thesis that nothing has changed in the Soviet empire is that the recent 'democratic' elections which resulted in several opponents of the régime being elected to the Soviet 'parliament' were conducted under conditions which guaranteed the continuing ascendancy of the Communist Party; that despite the reduction in armaments we don't know if Gorbachev is telling the truth about the strength of Soviet military forces; and that, as exemplified by the recent riots in Georgia, separatist aspirations are still suppressed by Soviet tanks as in Hungary in 1956 and Czechoslovakia in 1968.

Let's grant that all this is true. Does it support the proposition that those in the West, such as well-known former anti-Soviet hardliners like Reagan, George Kennan and Margaret Thatcher, have been fooled by a super conman and that everything that he has said and done which points to an unravelment of Soviet tyranny and paranoia is to be dismissed as so much duplicitious rhetoric, designed merely to persuade the West to drop its guard?

If such a proposition proves anything it is the unfitness of media gurus such as Alan Jones to keep the public informed about what is really going on in the world. They daily purvey over the airwaves and in print trivia, gossip and lowest-common-demoninator profundities at overblown rates of pay.

The very raison d'être of such people is the perpetuation of a populuist demonology decked out in clichés such as the leopard being unable to change its spots.

To believe that Gorbachev genuinely wants a freer, more open, more pluralistic society in the Soviet world and a less bellicose, because less apprehensive, world outside its borders does not involve any necessary belief in a 'change of heart'.

That may also be the case with Gorbachev, but it is not a condition of believing that he means it.

Gorbachev inherited the leadership of a stagnant, malfunctioning economy. The ailing, conservative Brezhnev, whose rule was characterised by nepotism and corruption, was succeeded towards the end of 1982, to the surprise of many Kremlin-watchers, by the former KGB chief, Yuri Andropov.

His ascendancy marked the real turning point in recent Soviet history, since he initiated the most far-reaching internal economic debate his country had seen.

But his reign was to be short; he died of a kidney complaint after little more than a year in office.

His reputation has been tarnished by his years at the head of the KGB, but the best informed opinion is that he was a highly intelligent man who clearly perceived the decay of the Soviet system and the urgent need for change.

Most importantly, he was the patron, mentor and promoter of the man who was to attempt to carry to fruition the policies which Andropov did not live long enough to get off the ground – Mikhail Gorbachev.

After Andropov died the Soviet gerontocracy, in its last kick, put one of its own, the nonentity Konstantin Chernenko, on the throne but he died after little more than a year in office. Then it was Gorbachev's turn.

Ah-hah, I can hear the cold-warriors crowing, so Gorbachev is the creature of a KGB chief, the suppressor of the Hungarian uprising of 1956! (I wonder if they would consider George Bush's stint as boss of the CIA and his involvement in the sleazy Irangate affair as any sort of a disqualification for leadership of the 'free world'?)

In any event, if Gorbachev had not initiated his reforms – and if they don't succeed – the whole Soviet pack of cards would be in danger of collapse. That won't mean we can all breathe more easily because there'll be no more threats from the East, but that Gorbachev will probably be succeeded by a conservative tyrant much more likely to revive the Cold War.

Implicit in Gorbachev's program is an admission that the Soviet system does not deliver goods to the supermarkets, that it produces a surly, restive, drunken, unproductive population and that such social ills are aggravated by the massive diversion of resources to a top-heavy military machine and to a repressive and inefficient bureaucracy.

The perception of these social cancers does not give Gorbachev free rein to do what he likes, overnight, to eliminate them. He does not exercise absolute power and, despite the clarity of his thinking, he does not wield a magic wand.

He knows the perils and the magnitude of the tasks he has undertaken. He can disappear overnight if he proceeds at a pace too fast for the entrenched bureaucracy whose power he must isolate and undermine.

Blemishes on the face of Soviet society, such as police oppression, limitations of the rights of ethnic minorities and a low standard of living, cannot, with the best will on the part of its new rulers, be erased overnight.

Instead of being so eager to highlight these remnants of the bad old days, as the cold-warriors are intent on doing, they should bear in mind that the face of Western democracy is also a bit spotty. They need go no further than to contemplate the horrors of the drug-dominanted, murder-prone, homeless underclass of Washington DC depicted by Max Walsh in his column in this paper last Monday.

Perhaps Alan Jones should confine his pontifications to rugby and other trivial pursuits which may appeal to him.

21 April 1989

98

IF THE MUD STICKS, DON'T EXPECT THEM TO WEAR IT

Auberon Waugh has argued, in the *Sydney Morning Herald*, that Salman Rushdie has no title to protection by the British authorities and that, if he wants protection, he should meet the cost himself.

The reason for Waugh's indifference to Rushdie's fate is that Rushdie, although he lives in England, has continued to assert the right to criticise what he considers to be reprehensible in British society. Waugh is saying that your right to the protection of British law is conditional on your conformity to censorship.

Censorship comes in many guises. Devotion to the allegedly fundamental democratic right to free speech is quite often very selective. I include under 'censorship' any pressure which deters a would-be communicator from saying or writing what he or she believes to be the truth.

The real reason why Justice Jim Staples was excised from the judicial system was that he exercised what he thought to be his right to say what he believed.

Gareth Evans, then Attorney-General, came up with a Uniform Defamation Bill in 1983, designed to replace the various State laws. Evans's bill would have made the infamous laws of defamation even more restrictive. Fortunately, it never became law. At the height of the debate, Evans attended a gathering where he was ruffled by his less than effusive reception. He warned that, although he was not among politicians who instruct lawyers to sue at the hint of a slur, we'd all better be careful what we said about him.

Fancy entrusting the reform of the law of defamation to a man so jealous of the reputation of public figures. And that is the main weakness in our present defamation laws – the excessive protection which they afford public figures.

As Robert Pullan points out in his excellent book, *Guilty Secrets*: 'Libel is a weapon of the elite, used by the people who have sought power, fame or money in the public arena, to punish attacks on their motives or performance.'

The defamation action has become a rort, a tax-free fringe benefit of the powerful. I do not agree with the practical immunity from criticism which our defamation laws confer on public figures and regard the law of defamation as the greatest single weapon of censorship in the armoury of the rich and powerful and corrupt.

Its most insidious effect is that it successfully cows publishers of books, newspapers, magazines, radio and television material into either not publishing information or comment which they think may attract a writ, or tamely paying up when they get one.

Amanda Lohrey's *The Reading Group* is another casualty of censorship by defamation action. I don't know what legal advice her publishers got, but it strikes me that an action based on the imputed resemblance between a fictional figure and a real person would by no means be certain to succeed.

At the News Unlimited conference in Sydney, which discussed implications of the apparently unstoppable spread of the Murdoch media empire, Barry Porter, federal president of the Australian Journalists' Association, said: 'The world is divided into two types of journalists: those who have worked for Rupert Murdoch and those who are about to.' I detect among many working journalists an unspoken self-imposed caveat on their public statements about Murdoch. Will he ultimately be the only newspaper proprietor one can work for in Australia?

The most chilling warning of the results of a media monopoly was uttered by Mia Doornaert, president of the International Federation of Journalists: 'The danger is not of direct censorship nor of direct control expressed through the imposition of proprietorial diktat – although this is increasingly likely, given the behaviour of some of the most colourful Western media owners – but that self-censorship among journalists will increase.'

Another great threat to freedom of expression is a deal between newspaper proprietors and political leaders in which the quid pro quo for political favour is an undertaking to treat a politician kindly in the proprietor's publications.

Who wouldn't like to have a transcript of the conversations between Neville Wran, Kerry Packer, Rupert Murdoch and Robert Sangster which preceded the grant of the highly lucrative Lotto franchise? Wran sold that proposition to his colleagues, most of whom had been brought up to believe that the 'capitalist press' was Labor's greatest enemy, with the argument that the grant of the franchise would ensure that Labor had some friends in the media who would give them a 'fair go'. And so they did.

The intertwining of political and business interests leads inexorably to subtle forms of censorship in which the loser is anyone who wants to know what is going on in the world.

Among the most fraudulent exercises of political power is censorship in the cause of so-called national security. The outstanding recent example was the *Spycatcher* case, in which Margaret Thatcher attempted to preserve secrets which must have been known to Soviet intelligence for decades. To their credit, the Australian judges put their foot down.

Now there are the memoirs of Eric Nave, a ninety-year-old Australian former naval commander and director in Victoria of ASIO. Nave claims that Churchill knew of the impending attack on Pearl Harbour before it occurred, but withheld the information from Roosevelt to make sure the United States was dragged into the war on Britain's side. Another possible construction is that Churchill told Roosevelt, but that the American president shared Churchill's view that a shock like Pearl Harbour was needed to jolt the American people out of their traditional isolationism.

Bodley Head withdrew its offer to publish the memoirs after a visit by representatives of the Ministry of Defence, which claimed that disclosure of something that happened nearly fifty years ago might damage national security.

An improvement in our defamation laws strikes me as the most important single contribution that can be made to the removal or at least lightening of the weight of censorship from which we suffer.

Above all, a distinction must be drawn between what may be said or written about ordinary citizens and about public figures. A public figure volunteers for public scrutiny while the life of an ordinary citizen is his own.

The 1964 judgment of the US Supreme Court in the case of *The New York Times* v. Sullivan should become the model for our own laws. Pointing out that erroneous statement is inevitable in free debate, the judgment established the rule that a public official cannot win a libel suit 'unless he proves that the statement was made with "actual malice" – that is, with knowledge that it was false or with reckless disregard of whether it was false or not'.

Since it is our public figures who are the principal beneficiaries of our present code, don't hold your breath waiting for them to change the law. That will happen only when there is a groundswell for a change.

30 March 1989

THE POLITICS OF PRETTINESS

If Ollie North ran for President tomorrow I get the impression that he would romp in. What are his qualifications? He has admitted that he has lied to Congress, to the US Attorney-General and the CIA. He has thumbed his nose at laws passed by Congress and justified his actions on the grounds that, being more patriotic than the legislators, he knows better than they do what is in the best interests of the country in keeping the Commies at bay. He has admitted, in fact practically boasted, that he shredded documents relevant to the investigation of the Iran–Contra scam.

And what has his grossly illegal conduct earned for him? The applause of a large section of the American people. The fact that this can happen in the US and come out almost by accident is disturbing enough. I hope that there is no nondescript junior officer in the KGB with the power to run his own private war. But then again, Gorbachev is no senile nincompoop who would let an underling get away with anything like that. The most disturbing aspect of the North affair is that it shows that there is nobody up there on the bridge. The Ship of State is like an unguided missile.

I proffer a suggestion that North could not have emerged from his criminal follies as a national hero if he had looked like Jimmy Durante instead of Glenn Ford. The clean-cut all-American boy can overcome the evidence of the smoking gun.

Which brings us to the larger question of the role of looks in political life. Could a Billy Hughes or a John Curtin be elected in this television era? Last Saturday night, I did a commenting stint for a commercial radio station in the central tally room at Canberra. After Hawke's victory had been conceded, Andrew Peacock made an appearance on the tally room floor. I use the words 'made an appearance' advisedly.

Having just emerged from the gaze of the cameras of one of the TV channels for which he had been performing, he was carefully made up and wearing his man-of-destiny look. He was interviewed by a herd of media sharks quite close to my table. His jaw was jutting, he showed his better profile to the media cameras which were now trained on him, and as he answered questions, his voice had dropped at least an octave from the one he uses in casual conversation. He was a small 'p' peacock.

What else but his handsomeness has kept him steadily ahead of John Howard in the personal popularity stakes? Most people who know Andrew should be aware that he is a pleasant enough, shallow poseur. Like him or not, there is a lot more than that to John Howard. But so close was the election result and so irrelevant some of the matters which evidently affect voting habits that it is possible to give credence to the view I heard expressed after the result became apparent that if Peacock had led the Libs in the campaign, they would have won.

It was a similar judgment on the other side of politics which induced the ALP to replace Bill Hayden with Bob Hawke on the eve of the 1983 elections. The gambit worked and confirmed the view I have expressed that appearance plays an inordinate, even dangerous, role in politics. In my view, Hawke is to Hayden much as Peacock is to Howard.

Appearance, via television, also plays an important role in international politics. Glasnost, which is translated in the West as 'openness', also bears the meaning 'publicity'. One of the aspects of the new policy is the availability of Soviet authorities – Gorbachev himself is the most visible of all Russian leaders. Glasnost has the twofold purpose: to bring to light and expose defects in the Soviet system, as part of Gorbachev's war against the stiflingly conservative Soviet bureaucracy, and also to convince the West that Russia is becoming more democratic and therefore less fearsome. It is no accident that the salesman of this strategy, who appears constantly on the world's TV screens, is a much more prepossessing figure than a suet-pudding Brezhnev or a porcine Khrushchev.

Gorbachev, whose birthmarked brow even provides an exotic gloss, comes across as an alert, civilised, eminently reasonable man who could pass as a member of any Western intelligensia. TV exalts image over content. The picture which meets our eye on the screen can largely obliterate, if it pleases us, the unpleasantness or vacuity of what is being said by the talking head.

If Bruce Ruxton did not look so avuncular, his fascistic outpourings would be even more obviously offensive than they are. And the appearance of our Prime Minister gazing with reverence at what his minders have obviously told him is a tree establishes his credentials as a conservationist more persuasively than a hundred words of his meandering prose.

Mind you, the primacy of the image can sometimes work on the side of the angels. Nixon's sinister five-o'clock shadow did more to bring him undone with the public than the exposure of his evil deeds. Paul Keating, who suffers from a similar handicap and is so portrayed by the cartoonists, may be obliged, if he is ever to make the top job, to shave every hour on the hour.

In a world dominated by the TV camera, the Max Gillies, the Moirs, the Mike Carltons become ever more precious creatures. Nearly every public figure is partly a figure of fun and those who constantly remind us of their ridiculous side do a great public service.

Sydney Morning Herald cartoonist, Moir's EIEIO number plate on Joh's jalopy bumping along towards Canberra did as much to trip up the old charlatan as the most erudite editorial. I commend to the electorate the adage: Handsome is as handsome does.

17 July 1987

THE DANGERS OF TRAVELLING BY CAB

I hope that the last charge that could be levelled against me, even by the not inconsiderable number of people who regard my views with some distaste, would be that of Pommophilia.

But I must confess to a grudging respect for (even an enjoyment of) the writings of some English journalists whose opinions make my gorge rise. One of these is Auberon Waugh, who makes Bob Santamaria sound like a raving leftie, but who is never boring and often hilariously entertaining.

Another is Paul Johnson, whom I met when he was still editor of the *New Statesman*, then the bible of the British Left, but who was already on his turn to the right as a result of a divine visitation on the road to Damascus. At that time he once dined at my table along with a few unreconstructed dissenters from the received wisdom of our times, and he was not too delighted with us.

He has for the past few years contributed a column on the

media to England's leading conservative weekly, *The Spectator* (until recently part of the Fairfax stable). His column oozes a Brahminish distaste for anything or anyone with a leftish taint and he exudes an unabashed reverence for Thatcherism. But he writes with panache and a certain splenetic bravura.

When I read either of these wordsmen I can dimly comprehend the pleasures of masochism. As they flog my cherished values their words give me an odd titillation.

This rather long preamble brings me to my point: why are our own conservative pundits, with a few conspicuous exceptions, such yobbos? The worst of them are on radio.

Let's start with the doyen of talk-back tedium, John Laws. Any masochistic tendencies I may have don't extend to a voluntary exposure of his program. But as I don't drive a car, I often find myself for short periods in a cab when Laws's lucubrations are cluttering the airwaves. He's obviously the cab drivers' darling and I think I know why.

He serves up a diet of mainstream banalities, dressed up by his scriptwriters as self-evident universal truths, uttered in the synthetic voice-over of the professional huckster. He offers potted wisdom to those who, like himself, can't be bothered thinking. The business of cab-driving is inimical to cerebration and makes some otherwise bright people receptive to the quick-fix nostrums in which Laws specialises.

On one of my recent cab journeys Laws was pontificating about homelessness. You guessed it: the homeless are feckless, anti-social, druggy dropouts who deserve to sleep on the streets. After letting this message sink in, he had the usual saver that not every homeless person fits this stereotype but the overwhelming impression created was that the homeless people who did not deserve their fate were as rare as hens' teeth.

To my delight, this cab driver, an intelligent Hungarian, did not buy the Laws message, pointing out that when he first arrived in this country there was an abundance of cheap accommodation where even the impoverished could at least get a roof over their heads but that this was no longer the case.

Our yobbo gurus are so predictable in their reactions to the issues of the day that I sometimes think there must be some intellectually down-market boutique where they all go to be fitted out with their shallow, reactionary opinions. There is really nothing surprising in the fact that Alan Jones wants a moratorium on the pursuit of unprosecuted war criminals in our midst. After all, few of them are likely to be lefties so why not let sleeping monsters lie?

The only surprising thing about redneck Ron Casey is that he is allowed to mouth his visigothic views on a 'Labor' radio station.

Recently Paul Johnson wrote a piece for the *Spectator* headed 'Why media folk are hated'. He instanced a jury award of £300 000 damages to Koo Stark, 'whose only crime was to have once had a fling with a young Royal', as demonstrating the British public's dislike for the media and its disapproval of the assumption, especially by the tabloids, that they 'can trample on the private lives of celebrities or indeed just ordinary people like a herd of elephants'.

So he supports changes proposed in the Thatcher Government's White Paper on broadcasting which would have the effect of diminishing the power of the media. Not only does he support restrictions on the showing on television of violence and what he considers porn, but he wants closest scrutiny of the veracity of TV documentaries. He is particularly concerned about the activities of a 'small though noisy left-wing minority among working journalists'.

It's not hard to imagine what Johnson would think of some of the disclosures of our investigative journalists on the ABC's *Four Corners*. Just below the surface of what he writes is a plea for increasing censorship of what he does not like in the media, mostly anything with a permissive or left-wing flavour.

Censorship of the media is a delicate issue and one calling for eternal vigilance. For example, I believe that anybody concerned with the preservation of freedom of speech should keep a watchful eye on the pursuit of Brian Toohey now being conducted by Gareth Evans.

This brings me back to my own distaste for the right-wing

ranters who occupy so much of our own air space. Let me hasten to add that I am not suggesting any increase in governmental intervention to suppress expressions of opinion on the air, no matter how distasteful they may be to my ears. Any society has a right to set up a code specifying what is unacceptable on the airwaves and to leave it to licensees to enforce such codes, but the political or moral or philosophical preferences of listeners or viewers should have no place in such codes and there should be a wide discretion to be offensive. After all, viewers and listeners can always switch off.

(I think anyone who has hired a cab temporarily should be entitled to ask the driver to switch off a program just as he or she should be entitled to ask the driver not to smoke during the hirer's journey.)

As to veracity, about which Paul Johnson is so concerned, there is more than ample protection in our over-protective defamation laws for those who consider themselves maligned, without having resort to more censorship.

So whatever we may think of them we just have to put up with the likes of John Laws, Alan Jones, Ron Casey – and Jim McClelland.

30 November 1988

THE CULTURAL CRINGE RETURNS

It's a long time since Bob Menzies left us to take his place in that special enclave in Heaven reserved for Anglo-Saxon gentlefolk, but the cultural cringe which he personified and sought to perpetuate is still alive and healthy in this country.

It is ironical that it should find a special niche in the columns of the newspaper which goes by the name of the *Australian*.

Last Saturday's issue of that paper featured a column by Greg Sheridan, lamenting what he sees as the mediocrity of contemporary Australian writing and confessing that 'one major reason why I read a great many of the books I do read is patriotic duty'.

He went on to praise some books by British authors he had recently read, and to declare that Australian works 'are so rarely of any genuine intellectual consequence'.

In the field of literature, I agree that there is no place for the virtue, favoured by our economists in the interests of correcting our balance of payments problem, which goes by the name of 'import replacement'.

If Australian literature needs the protection of an artificially fostered pious obligation to buy and read books merely because they are written by Australians about Australia, we cannot be said to have come of age culturally.

But a brief examination of the facts demonstrates that the assertion that Australian literature needs the prop of patriotism to survive and flourish is wildly untrue.

Sheridan confesses that he has not yet been able to don his patriotic hair-shirt and face up to plunging into Peter Carey's *Oscar and Lucinda*, which stares at him accusingly from his bookshelves.

Should he not ask himself whether it was patriotism which induced an international literary jury to award Carey's novel the Booker Prize, in a field which included the justifiably world-renowned Salman Rushdie?

He grits his teeth and reluctantly nibbles, out of patriotic duty, at one of Patrick White's novels, also glowering at him from his shelves, and is provoked into asking: 'Isn't there anyone else out there who finds Patrick White, well, turgid?' Once again, he might have asked himself whether Australianness had anything to do with this author's being awarded the Nobel Prize for literature by judges far away from this remote land.

This is not to suggest that an Australian work should be deemed to be of literary worth only if it is so adjudged by foreign literary pundits.

Such a yardstick would itself be a prime example of the cultural cringe.

But is he suggesting that the Booker and Nobel judging panels are a bunch of politicians who meet and say: 'Well, this year it is Brazil's – or India's, or Peru's, or Australia's – turn?'

If this is his opinion, I think he should have said so. In my view, his judgment of Australian literature is untenable unless he so asserts.

The State Library of NSW (whose Mitchell Library is running the excellent exhibitions People, Print and Paper, tracing the history of books and publishing in Australia) estimates that the Australian book market is dominated by home-grown writers and publishers.

Sheridan should ask himself who twists the arms of the purchasers of Australian books to compel them, free as they are with the choice of the world's best books, to buy these local products.

In the dog-eat-dog competition among publishers here and abroad, there are (as exposed recently in an instructive series in this paper by Robert Haupt) some obstacles to the free play of market forces in the literary domain.

But there is no protectionist policy in favour of local literary productions; Australian writers have to slug it out with the world's best.

If they write a poor book, they can bet it will be remaindered rather than read.

If their product is good, the word soon gets around, and it sells.

In general, ruthless market forces prevail in the literary arena.

Some of Sheridan's arguments have a certain plausibility. For example, who could cavil at his lament about the quality of political biography and autobiography in this country?

But surely this is a comment on the quality of our politicians, rather than of our writers.

You are not likely to get enthralling biographies of the mediocrities who have thronged our corridors of power; when such people write about themselves, they predictably put their nonentity on display.

England far surpasses us in this field because more interesting and accomplished people have been attracted to a life of politics there than here, and so write better autobiographies and provide better subjects for biographers.

It is true, as was suggested, that a lot of our non-fiction has been of poor quality.

But in recent years, I have not read much better non-fiction than Donald Horne's *The Education of Young Donald*, or David Marr's *Barwick*.

A discussion like this can easily degenerate into a rather meaningless catalogue which would establish nothing much more than what literature I value and what the *Australian*'s columnist does not.

But I think I can honestly say that the criterion of Australianness plays little part in my evaluation of what I read and what I eschew.

Patriotic duty is the poorest reason to buy or read a book. But perhaps Sheridan and I are in merely semantic disagreement. Patriotism is no bad thing, so long as it does not degenerate into jingoism.

But a natural interest in our own more talented writers, either of fiction or non-fiction, who seriously attempt to explain ourselves to ourselves, is a universal preoccupation which deserves a better name than patriotism, which too often carries the implication that one's own country is superior to others.

Why we are what we are, and how we got that way, is a subject which has little to do with patriotism.

Manning Clark and Donald Horne have more to tell us on these subjects than A. J. P. Taylor, Hugh Trevor-Roper or Malcolm Muggeridge, not because they are better writers (although I think they are just as good), but because they are naturally more interested in the subject and more knowledgeable about it than Anglocentric writers.

I confess that in my formative years, when the books I devoured were mostly by English writers, I was also a victim of the cultural cringe. I could not imagine that any writing other than that which emerged from the old centres of culture could be any good.

That was not true, as I have subsequently discovered. I would estimate that I am some forty years older than Sheridan and those have been the years in which Australian literature has truly blossomed. There is no excuse any longer for the view, implicit in his piece, that a book is not likely to be any good unless it comes from overseas, preferably from England.

Who needs the ghost of Bob Menzies haunting our bookshops?

27 January 1989

LEGISLATING AGAINST RACISM

During a visit to New York last October my wife and I took in a show by Jackie Mason, one of those Jewish stand-up comedians without whom the Big Apple could hardly function.

One of his jokes, told in a rich Brooklyn accent, went like this: 'I know this guy who is half Polish and half German. Boy, does he hate Jews. Trouble is, he can't remember why.'

The sheer irrationality of most racist prejudice is what makes it such an intractable social disease. The spraying of racist graffiti on the house of Mrs Irene Moss, a Federal race discrimination commissioner, and the firing of shots into the house of Mr Eddie Funde, the Australian representative of the African National Congress, are manifestations of a spate of racist activities in this country.

What is an appropriate community riposte to this ugly outbreak?

Article 4 of the International Convention on the Elimination of all Forms of Racial Discrimination, to which Australia is a signatory, obliges all parties to prohibit incitement to racial hatred and the dissemination of racist material.

But it's easier said than done. The Greiner government, with praiseworthy intent, has proposed amendments to the Anti-Discrimination Act of 1977, to prohibit public acts of racial vilification. It has drafted a bill to that effect and has circulated a discussion paper, including the bill, in the hope of stimulating public debate before submitting the bill to Parliament.

The bill has already aroused some uneasiness among civil libertarians and was one of the subjects of debate at the Writers' and Readers' Festival in the Domain.

Writers, with their experience of the limitations on plain speaking imposed by our defamation laws (which should be renamed laws for the protection of crooks in high places) and with the example of the threatened pulping of Amanda Lohrey's book *The Reading Group*, are chary of an increase in Government powers to censor written material. The history of publishing in this country is studded with heavy-handed bureaucratic interventions in the dissemination of ideas.

The Government's proposals seek to pay regard to 'a balancing of the right to free speech and the right to a dignified and peaceful existence free from racist harassment and vilification'.

Rightly, the proposed legislation does not set out to prohibit racist jokes. Many of these are pretty offensive, but you may as well try to prohibit men from getting erections. Unenforceable legisation is always bad legislation.

So what will the proposed legislation prohibit? Public acts which will become subject to penalty will include 'any form of communication to the public, including speaking, writing, printing, displaying notices, broadcasting, telecasting, screening and playing of tapes or other recorded material . . . which promotes or expresses hatred towards, serious contempt for, or severe ridicule of, a person or group of persons on the ground of the race of the person or member of the group'.

Spot on, most enlightened people would say, but let's have a closer look at the implication of this praiseworthy code. In the first place, detection of such acts as spraying graffiti on to, or spraying bullets into, people's homes will not be any easier. Most such ghouls do their dirty work in the dark or when the chance of detection is minimal. They are unlikely to be deterred merely by the fact that their offences will be specifically prohibited by statute. This is not an argument against the bill's enactment, but a caution against extravagant expectations of its effect.

I also see the danger of a lawyer's picnic resulting from the proposed legislation. The bill contains a saving clause exempting from its reach 'a public act, done reasonably and in good faith, for academic, artistic, scientific research or religious purposes or for other purposes in the public interest . . .'.

A mad mullah to whom all religious belief other than Islamic fundamentalism is a road to perdition could successfully invoke the protection of this section for the most poisonous attacks on Judaism, Christianity or even atheism. Look at Salman Rushdie's experience with *The Satanic Verses*. Some of history's greatest crimes have been committed in the name of religion – including the religion of Marxism.

And a lot of the cleverest and most dangerous forms of racism will not be caught by such an enactment. Despite his disavowals I believe that the immigration policy announced by John Howard last year was a subliminal ploy for the votes of Australia's unfortunately numerous, sometimes almost unconscious, racists.

'One nation' was intended to be understood as one white nation and the limit Howard proposed on our intake of immigrants was intended to apply primarily to Asian immigrants. There are more ways to appeal to racist prejudice than to resort to the redneck crudities of a Ron Casey. To his credit, Greiner has distanced himself from Howard's shoddy opportunism on this issue.

So, after a bit of agonising, I finally come down on the side of Greiner's proposed legislation but without holding any wild hopes that it will produce the sudden death of racism in our country.

7 February 1989

THE LESSON OF HARMONY STREET

Western Australia's Premier, Brian Burke, recently opined that the majority of Australians were racists. I've not felt any particular admiration for Burke in the past but I give him full marks for saying something which his electorate would not like to hear. It is not generally considered good politics to tell home truths to voters.

Although there is no such thing as a blood test to establish that the virus of racism infects any particular person and most would deny the charge with the tell-tale alibi 'some of my best friends are Blacks or Orientals or Jews', my lifelong observations compel me to side with Burke on this subject.

And you strike racism in some unexpected places.

Recently I was asked by an old friend to give an after-dinner speech at the annual dinner of a prestigious professional group of which he is a member. I am averse to the sort of tailored-to-please speech which you'd expect from one of Harry M. Miller's stable pros. So I gave a frank but, to my mind, unprovocative talk on a subject which had recently been put to me by an interviewer who did not err on the side of tact: 'Is the world you will soon be leaving a better or worse place than the one you entered so long ago?'

I was heard in polite silence, even drawing a laugh or two, and greeted with mild applause. But something in my general tone must have raised the suspicion in some of my audience that some dangerous opinions might lurk in my breast. After I sat down the chairman suggested that some of the guests might like to ask me some questions.

The first question put to me was as to my reaction to the dramatic change in our ethnic mix which hits anybody in the face as he or she strolls through the streets of our major cities.

No overtly racist terms were used by my questioner. But it was impossible not to detect in the way his question was framed that I was being invited to express disapproval of the dilution of our once-predominantly Anglo-Celtic identity. If he did not expect a reply in the redneck tones of a Bruce Ruxton or a Ron Casey, he at least hoped for a cold douche on multiculturalism à la Geoffrey Blainey. Perhaps even a word like 'mongrelisation' would not have been considered over the top.

He and some others present were obviously disappointed by my reply. I said I welcomed racial diversity and that the old Anglo-Celtic predominance had had a lot to do with the boring provincialism which had characterised Australia up to the past few years. I evidently rubbed salt into a few wounds by adding that I found the oriental physiognomy generally more attractive than the occidental and that current ethnic trends in this country presaged a better-looking Australia.

A life of contention has inured me against hostile interjection but in this blandly privileged gathering I was somewhat taken back by a waspish comment from one of the women present: 'What an appalling answer.' A man sitting next to her then challenged me: 'Would you abolish our flag and Anzac Day?'

To which I replied that in these troubled times those two questions were low on my list of preoccupations.

When we got home my wife and I discussed this incident. There was nothing surprising to us in the fact that well-educated, prosperous people of a naturally conservative bent are not immune to the most vulgar prejudice. But this was the sort of gathering that you would have expected at least to be able to suppress in public its displeasure at hearing views which it found abhorrent. My wife speculated on whether such conduct could be expected in a similar gathering in, say, London or New York or whether it was just another example of Australian provincialism.

I hasten to add that several of the guests approached me afterwards and one complimented me on my display of anti-racism. 'As a Jew,' he said, 'I am always glad to hear ALL racism condemned.'

Two days after this incident there appeared in the *Sydney*

Morning Herald a heart-warming story, illustrated by a photograph, headed 'harmony on the street where races meet'. The photograph showed six adjoining houses on Agar Street, Marrickville, and some of their inhabitants. Two of the families were Australian-born, two Portuguese, one Greek and one Indonesian.

The story was a tale of friendly, even affectionate neighbourly relations between these people of such diverse cultural backgrounds. The street also houses Yugoslavs and Italians. One Australian resident described the Yugoslav neighbours as 'lovely people' and mentioned that when he went shopping at the local Greek deli he tried to order his groceries in Greek. 'They love you for it,' he said.

It would be a safe bet that at the gathering which I addressed the overwhelming majority of the guests would have been residents of the affluent eastern or northern suburbs.

A chart attached to the *Sydney Morning Herald* story, derived from recent census figures, disclosed that the number of Greeks, Italians, Lebanese, Vietnamese, Yugoslavs and other ethnic groups living in those leafy purlieus is minuscule.

The picture is quite different in suburbs like Marrickville, Leichhardt and Fairfield. Could it be that there is a little parable about racism in this ethnic distribution? A big element in racist prejudice is fear of people who are different. Perhaps this fear is at least attenuated by propinquity. As we get to know people from an alien background and of obviously different physiognomy we may make the startling discovery that they are people just like ourselves. Perhaps that is the lesson of Agar Street, Marrickville.

18 November 1987

A CABBIE STIRS THE MELTING POT

One of my minor hobbies is cab-drivers. If I step into a cab and the radio is purveying the lucubrations of Alan Jones or John Laws, I don't attempt to start a conversation but I know that I will probably get an earful anyway from the driver of the received wisdom of those gurus of the airwaves.

That, to use a current buzz word, is the downside of the cabbie.

But every now and then you strike a gem. After a recent session of a little modest punditry of my own on a commercial radio station, I boarded a cab and in the short journey to my house I enjoyed the company of a delightful man.

Detecting an accent which I did not recognise – a challenge which I find almost as irresistible as a good port – I asked him where he came from. 'From Latvia via Queensland,' he said.

Thinking that the answer to my next question would tell me all I needed to know about him I asked: 'Why did you leave Queensland?' I though Joh would at least rate a mention and I would be able to place my cabbie's politics.

'The mosquitoes,' he replied. 'If there was only one of them in my street, it would find me and ignore my wife sitting beside me.'

We were soul-mates immediately, as that has also been exactly my experience. We were skin-brothers.

He had fled not so much from Latvia as from Europe – 'because every nation hates every other nation'.

I began to air some of my knowledge of ethnic idiosyncracies. I told him I had heard that the Finns were the biggest boozers in the northern hemisphere. 'After the Latvians,' he replied.

He attributed this national quirk to the fact that the country

118

had been dominated for 700 years by the Germans, who had built a pub on every street corner.

'But they only wanted to make money out of us. The Russians wanted to slit our throats.'

This was said factually, unbitterly, as a bald statement of the difference between two national attitudes to his people. I got a strong impression that he could not be bothered hating anybody.

My mind went back to the time when the first 'Balts' arrived in Australia. I recall them as among the first waves of post-war immigrants.

The stereotype of the Balt, especially to those like me on the left of politics, was of a fascistic, anti-Semitic reactionary. This was primarily because they were fleeing from the Russians.

But there was no whiff of hate from this laconic, mild-mannered, humorous man. He preferred Australian football to Rugby 'because there's less chance of them killing each other'.

As I got out of the cab, I asked him why he liked Australia: 'Because it's not as bad as everywhere else,' he replied.

Most national stereotypes are wrong or at least grossly over-simplified. I must confess that my own rough-and-ready picture of the 'average Pole' had been of a hard-drinking Catholic anti-Semite.

Recently we needed the services of a painter to paint our little shack in the mountains. My wife managed to find a Pole who turned out to be the best house painter (after my father) whom I have encountered.

On the first day, after he had been up on the roof for three hours in blazing sunshine, he descended his ladder at lunchtime and I asked him if he would like a beer.

He turned out to be a teetotaller. I got talking to him and he also turned out to be a Seventh Day Adventist. During the war, his family had given shelter to Jews. So much for my image of your average Pole.

The Polish painter recalled my father to mind. He used to tell me stories of his own father, whom I never met and who had been what was known in those days as an Orangeman, that is a Catholic-hating Ulsterman, the best (or worst) example of which is the Rev Ian Paisley.

Dad's father had savoured the bile of Ulster's hates and nothing pleased him more than to go into town on 17 March and jeer at the Micks in the annual St Patrick's Day Procession.

If he came home with a bloody nose, he regarded it as an honourable wound earned on the field of sectarian battle.

In socially healthy climes distant from their source, such prejudices gradually lose their strength, even though they may never totally disappear.

My father married a Catholic woman and, although I always suspected that he was a closet atheist and I never knew him to go to church, he adhered to his marriage promise to allow the children to be brought up as Catholics. It was none of his doing that we all ultimately abandoned the faith.

The notion that in inviting as permanent settlers in our country people of alien cultures with prejudices embedded by centuries of conditioning we are importing foreign poisons which will pollute the pure Anglo-Saxon stream is a vast exaggeration.

Recently I witnessed a little scene which movingly illustrated the falsity and meanness of the notion of unassimilability.

My wife and I were driving through Stanmore a little after ten in the morning.

We became aware of a long procession of children in, I would estimate, the eight to ten years age group, walking towards us on the footpath, shepherded by adults who were obviously their teachers.

They were apparently from the same school and were being taken on some excursion or other.

We realised gradually that the procession consisted of a veritable United Nations of kids. They were of all colours and nationalities.

They were, as well as the unmistakably Australian, oriental, Lebanese, Greek and indefinable black faces. Many of the diverse nationalities were holding hands.

They were acting as though it was the most natural thing in the world that they did not all look alike.

That, I thought, is the face of the Australia of the future. And, *pace* Bruce Ruxton and Geoffrey Blainey, I believe that will not be a bad thing.

20 May 1987

THE GREAT AUSSIE MYSTERY

When the Australian Institute of Political Science chose the weekend of 19-20 March for its conference in Canberra on the subject 'What Does It Mean To Be An Australian in 1988?', it could not have been expected to know that that would be, according to your political proclivities, a time for jubilation or weeping and gnashing of teeth [The NSW state election was held during that weekend].

But the proceedings would certainly be enlivened if, on the Sunday morning after the election, they could produce Barrie Unsworth and Nick Greiner and put the question to each of them.

I would imagine that answers might vary considerably as between, on the one hand, Arvi Parbo, Peter Abeles, Alan Bond and Kerry Packer and, on the other, a single mother living in Mt Druitt. She would be able to testify, as would Nick and Barrie, that the answer depends a great deal on whether you are a winner or a loser.

Perhaps Rupert Murdoch could be asked the question. I suspect he might reply that when you are on top you don't feel much different whether you are an Australian or an American, but it is good business to claim to be both.

In any event, there was an all-star cast at the conference and, as I was asked to attend but chose instead the Adelaide Festival, I now proffer my modest contribution.

One of the problems about being a columnist is that words you have long forgotten can rise up to smite you. In a recent magazine article, I was reminded that I once wrote in a column in this paper: 'I believe that there is an identifiable kit of shared attitudes, sufficient to distinguish most Australians from, say, most Americans or Britishers and so justify the use of the term [Australians].'

That could be taken to mean that I accept that there is what I really regard as a metaphysical illusion: an Australian identity. All I meant to convey, and I confess that I expressed it with imprecision, was that there is a type who is recognisably and unmistakably Australian.

Barry Humphries has expressed this truism much more graphically than I but, I believe, much more unkindly. Every people produces caricatures of itself.

An editorial in the British publication *The Economist* of January 23 last, headed Take It Easy Oz, deals, inter alia, with what it calls 'The Phoney Identity Crisis'.

The writer suggests:

It will be easier for Australians to come to terms with the world once they have come to terms with themselves. If the Bicentenary binge promotes this, so much the better. The misplaced endeavour, however, is the search for an identity. It is horribly fashionable. Practically every book on Australia published this past year seems to have dwelt on the need for a national identity.

Romantics have long exaggerated the significance of the outback, Australian politicians have introduced idiotic national anthems, and film-makers have played fast and loose with history to propagate a view of Australia that fits the desired self-image. They are wasting their time. A contrived national identity will be a bogus one.

I could not agree more. The question: 'What is an Australian?' strikes me as about as meaningful as the old sophomoric game we all play at some times of our lives: 'What is the meaning of life?'

I never found the answer to that one but I have discovered

that life is worth living and worth trying to live well even if it has no meaning. Life is its own justification.

Similarly, I believe that we can absorb into our way of life and our culture whatever may be unique or special about our background, our history, our climate or whatever without becoming or wanting to become a distinct specimen of the general species homo sapiens.

To put it another way, we might all ask ourselves the question: 'With whom do I identify?' The countryman is more likely to identify with farmers everywhere than with Australian city intellectuals who feel uncomfortable unless there is bitumen under their shoes.

A person of literary tastes tends to identify with people of a similar bent and may feel quite alienated from or at least indifferent to the sort of person who is described as a 'typical Aussie'. There is an international clerisy which never feels especially Australian or English or French or American or Russian.

Our leading citizen, the Prime Minister, Mr Hawke, would, I sometimes feel, prefer to be Greg Norman or Allan Border, but just because he enjoys great popularity with the 'average Australian' does his known adulation of great sportsmen represent the norm and justify a sweeping classification of Australians as a nation of sports-lovers?

Even if that were true, there is a lot more to most of us than that. The best that can be said on that score is that because we enjoy more fine weather than most countries, sport tends to loom larger here than elsewhere. It would be just as true to categorise the Russians as a nation of chess-players because the predominance of freezing weather there fosters indoor diversions.

A national identity is often little more than a national stereotype. [See the previous piece on our Polish painter, which encourages some scepticism about Barry Humphries's attempt to portray us as a race of Les Pattersons].

I have found that affinities based on your immediate locality are often more powerful than national ties. There are many islands of atypicality in most countries. For example, New York is regarded by most Americans who don't live there as a national aberration, while those who live in the Big Apple regard themselves as New Yorkers rather than Americans.

Lamentably, the world cultural trend is towards homogenisation rather than national individuality. In the spheres of design, production and entertainment, international trends to set the tone cross national boundaries.

I expect that the gathering in Canberra next weekend will provide plenty of good, clean fun and, if it were not for the enticements of lovely little Adelaide, I would probably be there to join in the frolic.

But don't hold your breath for the definitive answer to the question: 'What is an Australian?'

Anyway, does it matter all that much? I'll settle for a multiplicity of identities.

18 March 1988

Even Death
MIGHT HAVE ITS PERILS

As Margaret Jones remarked on this page last Friday, this is the time of the year when even columnists become frivolous. When the politicians have closed the shop for the holidays, when the stores are displaying all those gewgaws which will be bought this week and tucked away forever in a drawer next week, when office parties transform sexual harassment into harmless flirtations and the advertisers are making more and more money out of flapdoodle, we pundits tend to catch the contagion and shed our customary solemnity.

When a septuagenarian like me reads, 'Death is the ultimate negative patient health outcome,' you wouldn't think it would amuse him, but I nearly died laughing. I put it down to the season. (This solemn observation by some pompous American scientist was singled out for ridicule in a recent copy of *New Yorker* magazine.)

Although by the time Christmas and New Year are over, some of us could do with a short period of total abstinence (say, a day), I should like to deliver a little homily in defence of conviviality.

This is prompted by another piece which appeared in this paper last week titled *Happy Days – What's Your Poison?*

I suspect that the writer had his tongue firmly in his cheek and that the article was intended as a send-up of those medical narks whose services are always available to damp down any tendency people may have to enjoy themselves.

As I read of the possibly dire consequences of more than one or two drinks, I wondered how it was that the ultimate negative patient health outcome had not overcome me some fifty years ago.

How is that my stomach, my heart, my liver, my brain, my pancreas seem all to be functioning reasonably well after so many years of foolish indulgence? One medical luminary is quoted as saying: 'It's a poison, so I can't see how you can argue that it is good for you.'

If the doctors are to be taken literally, my continued presence on this earth is an optical illusion. Dear doctors, such intemperance (the word means more than just getting pissed) does your cause no good.

Remember the boy who cried wolf. When young people observe from empirical experience that the dire forebodings of their elders do not eventuate, they are inclined to regard *all* the advice that they tender as being dispensable.

I wonder how many people's feet have been set on that path by their discovery after a few years of addiction to a common youthful practice that their eyesight was as good as ever.

Unquestionably, there are perils in drinking. So are there in being born, in breathing, in crossing the road, in indulging in sex, in watching TV, in getting married, in being Minister for Sport. And, if you believe in Hell, there are perils still ahead of you in that ultimate negative patient health outcome.

As John Stone might put it, the worst is yet to come. These reflections recalled to mind some other terroristic tactics employed to keep the young out of danger when I was growing up.

I remember being at the beach with my parents on those searing Melbourne summer days, lolling around impatiently on the sand for at least an hour after lunch, gazing longingly at the water, dying to dive in for a cooling douche but not daring to, since I had been warned that, if I did, my lunch would turn into a hard lump in my stomach and I would sink like a stone.

I knew also that if I accidentally or carelessly swallowed grape pips I would get appendicitis, with even graver consequences from engorging the stones of the larger fruits.

I knew better than to stand under a tree when lightning was about or to drink water or any other beverage while eating. As for having a shower when I had a cold, I soon learnt that was a prescription for doom. Better dirty than dead.

The skylarking young have sometimes been prone to roll their eyes into a momentary squint. Prudently, I eschewed that practice just in case the wind changed. If that happened when your eyes were out of their normal position, you would become cross-eyed for life.

Bob Hawke obviously never fell for that one. Perhaps, on reflection, it is not a fatal loss for the young to have to fight their way to enlightenment through a mire of crap.

The gradual process of shedding implanted shibboleths and superstitions and misinformation may help to induce a healthy scepticism about all received knowledge and thus stimulate the critical faculties.

After this outburst of seasonally induced levity I feel I must get back to basics.

While out on a little jaunt over the weekend I noticed some new bright green DMR signposting on the road leading from the airport to the Pagewood–Maroubra area, directing the public how to find their way to Eastgardens. Eastgardens is not a suburb but a huge, recently opened supermarket on the old Pagewood site.

Off-hand, I cannot recall any such government-installed instructions on how to find a supermarket. Mostly they are too ugly to miss, anyway.

As its brutish mass loomed into view with its mock-Grecian columns at the main entrance and the message emblazoned on its roof top that it is a Westfield project, the thought occurred to me that the proprietors of a shopping complex which exists only by grace and favour of the Wran Government would regard it as par for the course that its location should be advertised by that Government's successor.

Readers of this column may recall that a few weeks ago I told the tale of the divestment by special Act of Parliament of the Land and Environment Courts' jurisdiction to decide, according to the Wran Government's vaunted environmental legislation, whether the development should be allowed to proceed or not.

But surely it is fruit for the sideboard for Westfield's Mr Lowy to get a free plug at the taxpayer's expense as well?

I'll withdraw this unseasonably sour comment if I can be convinced that Mr Lowy contributed to the DMR for the erection of the signs.

24 December 1987

How vile prejudice
WAS DISPELLED WITH GOOD GRACE

The Christmas season we have just endured was, for me, the usual predictable occasion. But on a Christmas Eve 10 years ago an event occurred which changed my life.

A woman whom I did not then know was doing her final Christmas shopping at Grace Bros in Bondi Junction. Her eye was caught by a skinny black and white kitten in a cage and she asked the saleswoman: 'What becomes of that kitten if you can't sell it?' The saleswoman replied: 'I can't even give it away.'

On an impulse, the shopper replied: 'I'll take it.' She took it home and, out of deference to its provenance, called it Grace.

A few months later, when Grace was still a nondescript little alley-cat type, her owner and I met. During the brief courtship which culminated in our marriage a few months later, I must have made it pretty clear that not only was I not captivated by Grace, cats in general were not my cup of tea.

My mind goes back even further to a faded print which used to hang in the hallway of my childhood home, depicting a plump Rosetti-ish maiden with her hand on the head of a pampered dog at which she is gazing with treacly devotion while a dandified suitor pays court to her.

The caption on this very Victorian scene was 'Love me, love my dog'.

It was soon made clear to me by my putative wife that the same deal applied to our relationship: If you want me you'll have to cop Grace as well.

That was the beginning of my conversion to the ranks of cat lovers. Until then, I had had an aversion to cats. From boyhood I had always owned a dog and, never having observed the affectionate relationship which can develop between a dog and a cat which have been brought up together from an early age, I'd come to regard the two species as natural enemies. Out of solidarity with dogs I had unthinkingly adopted their view of cats. In short, my prejudice against cats, like most prejudices, was firmly anchored in ignorance.

Grace, the ugly duckling, blossomed into a beauty – sleek, dignified and charming. After a few weeks of her company she had won me.

I love the unsentimental independence of cats, which is often mistaken for unfriendliness. You can't cajole a cat, as you can a dog. They do things in their own time and according to their own schedule. But their strongest characteristic is their conservatism. They like a steady routine. They are firm adherents to the status quo.

Ours is a household where very young children are seldom seen. But on Christmas Day, an eighteen-month-old nephew of my wife's spent the night there with his mother. His gurglings and cupboard openings and the attention he attracted constituted a grave disturbance to Grace's routine. Her displeasure was patent.

Next morning, observing that the child was still there, she indicated her disapproval by leaping over a fence into a neighbour's garden. We had planned to leave early that day for our modest mountain retreat, to which Grace always accompanied us, albeit reluctantly, for she dislikes the car trip. Once there, though, she purrs with contentment.

She usually keeps an eye peeled for tell-tale signs of impending departure, such as the packing of bags, and we have developed strategies to frustrate her efforts to take evasive action.

But on this occasion, though she had been given no warning of our intentions, she was so cheesed off by the interruption of her usual placid routine – caused by the presence in her house on Christmas Day of an unusually large number of people, especially a child – that she defied our attempts to capture her.

She dodged from one (unoccupied) neighbour's house to another all day. We were forced to delay our departure until the next day, when she had regained her composure.

This recalled a previous occasion when we moved from one house to another in Sydney. During the trauma of the removalist's operations in clearing the contents of the house, we left Grace locked away on a verandah.

When the time came to carry her to the car and to her new home, my wife picked her up on the verandah and carried her through the now-empty house. I have never observed such a look of astonishment and consternation on any creature's countenance as when Grace surveyed a scene which, the last time she had looked at it, had been occupied by tables and chairs and beds and pictures but which was now entirely empty.

Some of my friends have baited me, a known anti-conservative, for my devotion to this most conservative of creatures. But I draw a distinction between conservatism and conservatives. I've found some people whose politics and philosophy are anathema to me to be among the most attractive people I have known.

On the other hand, I have found some people who were apparently on my political wavelength to be quite unlikeable, especially that not infrequent type of radical who loves humanity but can't stand people.

This is not a plea for a proposition that charm outweighs principle and it hasn't much to do with the evaluation of the merits of cats anyway.

'A cat may look at a king', as Lewis Carroll remarked. They are certainly no respecters of human self-importance, as Grace demonstrated on the day after Christmas.

31 December 1987

Reflections
ON LIFE, DEATH AND TOLERANCE

Until we get old we tend to regard death as something that happens to other people. The most persuasive reminder that none of us is exempt comes when we attend the funeral of a coeval.

These days that is happening to me more often. Recently I was asked by the son of an old friend to say a few words or, as it is ceremonially called, to 'deliver the eulogy' at his father's funeral service. I accepted that rather sombre task because I had been very fond of his father.

He was a former judge singularly free of the blemishes which diminish the appeal of so many lawyers – pomposity, narrowness of interests, overestimation of their importance.

The quality of the man is illustrated by a comment I heard him make years ago at a slightly bibulous gathering which included a few practitioners of his trade: 'What a lawyer needs above all else is a critical wife. In that respect I have been freakishly fortunate.' It was said affectionately and gratefully with his wife standing by his side.

I first met him as a struggling barrister when I was a struggling solicitor. I was immediately captivated by his charm, his wit and his humanity. Our paths diverged and I did not see him for many years. But a few years before his death I renewed contact with him, and, though he was in failing health, I was delighted to find his spirit was undiminished.

Throughout the period of our friendship I knew that he was a practising Catholic and he knew I was an atheist. It made no difference to our affection for each other.

But I must confess to having felt something like a trespasser when I was taken into a room alongside the altar at the lovely old church where the ceremony was to take place. There I was introduced to the priest who was to conduct the Requiem Mass.

Even holy men read newspapers, I thought; if he has ever read my column in this paper, he must know my form. He greeted me with what I took to be some hauteur, but as I was leaving the room to wait in the body of the church for the ceremony to begin he murmured in my ear in a mellifluous Irish voice: 'I'm a regular reader of your column. I don't always agree with you but I always enjoy it.' I thought it was a gracious way to put me at ease in my unaccustomed surroundings.

I had forgotten how much movement is involved in a Requiem Mass, but as there were other former judges of my vintage there, I did not feel all that self-conscious about my creaking joints as I kept standing up and sitting down between the hymns and the prayers. I was quite moved by the singing of a choir of adolescent girls.

All in all, the occasion was a reminder to me of the comforts of religion and the reasons why people cling to beliefs which I cannot share. Good luck to them! But the sharpest memory I took from the occasion was of the tolerance of the priest. And why, after all, should there be any antipathy between the sincere atheist and the sincere believer? The real enemies are moral indifference, fence-sitting and apathy.

A short time ago I wrote a piece in this paper in which I referred to the letters I get from religious people who are sorry for me for missing out on the comforts they derive from their

131

faith. I remarked: 'I invariably give them a soft answer, because I do not wish to kick away anybody's props.'

This remark provoked a sour rebuke from a pastor of the Uniting Church in Australia: 'How patronising and arrogant can one be?' That was not the way my comment was intended.

I was once an ardent proselytiser for atheism, like Phillip Adams, who is much better at it than I ever was. But while I still believe it is cowardly to conceal your atheism, and I have always refused to swear by Almighty God, I now regard it as uncivil to confront people about strongly held beliefs from which they draw comfort and which cause no harm to anyone else. This dispensation does not extend, of course, to anti-social religious fanatics like Ayotollah Khomeini, Jerry Falwell or Fred Nile. I regard such people as anti-life.

There are varying levels of belief, ranging from certainty to what is really not much more than a vague hope. I can't help noticing that even those who have been persuaded that life is merely a preparation for the beatific vision are in no hurry to shuffle off this mortal coil, but cling to life as stubbornly as those of us who believe that is all there is.

There is in the Christian world, fortunately, none of that Islamic fervour to embrace death in the service of Allah, which accounted for thousands of pointless deaths in the cruel Iran-Iraq war.

I hold the view that the basic underpinning of religious belief is an understandable reluctance to accept the finiteness of life. That is what keeps religion alive, even if it does nothing to keep people alive.

It was an odd feeling to find myself in a pulpit, from which I delivered my tribute to my old friend. But the solemn finality of death expunged from my mind all thoughts of the philosophical differences which separated me from those around me.

John Donne, a clergyman and one of our greatest poets, deserves the last word: 'Any man's death diminishes me, because I am involved in mankind. And therefore never send to know for whom the bell tolls; it tolls for thee.'

23 March 1989

A BLEEDING HEART? – MAYBE

Some of the mail I get is from people who want to reconvert me to a belief in the God I rejected fifty-five years ago. One such letter, written in a kindly tone by a woman who had just heard a replay of an interview I had had with the ABC's Carolyn Jones a few months earlier, suggested that I was still a believer without realising it. Her theme was that it was just not possible to adhere to an ethical view of human responsibility, which she adjudged me to have, without continuing supernatural guidance.

I have regarded the concept of God as irrelevant to human affairs for so long that on such occasions I have to dredge up from the depths of my memory bank the reasons why, at the age of seventeen, I turned my back on God forever.

I don't bash my correspondents' ears with those reasons nor do I propose to assault my readers' patience with them. I reply generally in a tone of you go your way and I'll go mine.

But the question remains: are people who have had an early religious conditioning more likely than those who have not had one to retain an ethical standard which affects strongly the conduct of their lives even when God has been extruded from their philosophy?

I believe the answer is yes, although not primarily because of the supernatural ingredient in such an upbringing. At a time when sweeping structural changes to the educational system are on the agenda, serious thought should be given, not to reinstating God in an increasingly secularised society, but to providing some ethical underpinning for the young before they embark on their post-school lives.

Every now and then, some survey comes up with statistics on belief and non-belief in a Supreme Being.

Although none of these surveys gainsays the fact that there

has been a drastic and continuing decline in religious practice in the past fifty years, a surprisingly small proportion of people surveyed is prepared to declare itself atheistic or agnostic.

A more realistic question would be: what part, if any, does God play in determining your conduct?

If honest answers were given, the figures for that question would I suspect be much more negative than for the simple question: do you believe in God?

It takes a little thought and often a little courage to express dissent from a view held by a large majority of your fellows. The easiest answer is to express agreement with the majority, especially if it does not interfere with the way you conduct your life.

I believe that people who live good lives do so, not because of the incorporeal myths with which they have been inculcated but because, in so-called Christian societies, they have imbibed the Judeo-Christian ethic which accompanies such a conditioning. Most people who shed the myths continue to retain the ethic.

The most important ingredient in this ethic is concern for those less fortunate than ourselves. Its opposite is the I'm-all-right-Jack social Darwinism which is in the ascendant increasingly today.

If the Judeo-Christian ethic depended for its influence on a belief in God, you would expect non-believers to have a lower code of morals than believers. On the contrary, many of the villains I have known have expressed a belief in God. This is a further proof that such a belief *by itself* has little to do with human conduct.

Children attending non-denominational schools usually get rudimentary 'scripture' lessons which are not compulsory. But they get nothing like the intense form of indoctrination which characterises the denominational, especially Catholic, schools.

I agree with most of the Judeo-Christian ethic, shorn of its supernatural trappings.

I can see no reason why we can't have one without the other. Parents who want their children to have both send them, if they can afford the fees, to denominational schools. Those who can't afford it send them to schools where there is little emphasis on religious teaching.

I wonder if any thought is being given by those engaged in plans to restructure the education system to introducing into the curriculum for senior students a subject on ethics independent of theology.

I'm not suggesting that any limitation should be placed on religious teaching in those schools where it is part of the package which parents are buying. But in other schools such a subject might provide some guidance to the young on how to conduct their lives.

I get the impression from what I read about the attitude of today's school kids that there is a growing respect among them for financial success, that the Alan Bonds and Rupert Murdochs and the money-market yuppies and the carefully managed sports heroes like Pat Cash are becoming their role-models.

Moral inculcation may strike today's hard-headed pragmatists as a luxury which society cannot afford. But such a course could also, if properly taught, expand the boundaries of youthful knowledge by including a history of the world's religions and ethical systems and their relationships to the economies in which they have been and are being practised.

Let me stress that the course I am suggesting would bear no resemblance to Fred Nileism, with its accent on sin and guilt. It should be factual and scientific and calculated to arouse the interest of inquiring young minds.

Some years ago, when I was a practising politician, I coined the phrase 'the politics of the warm inner glow', to describe the actions and attitudes which achieved nothing much but to increase the righteous feelings of those who expound them.

The phrase has entered the political lexicon but it is now used as a term of abuse for those who believe sound economic management can co-exist with measures for the amelioration of the lot of the underprivileged.

In short, ethical considerations have become unfashionable in politics and carry the stigma of sentimental unreality. At the risk of being branded a 'bleeding heart', I suggest that morality should have a leading role in the conduct of our polity.

21 April 1988

An Idea
WHOSE TERM HAS NOT YET COME

The term 'motherhood issue' was made fashionable by journalists to describe a political proposal which nobody would dare to oppose because it is based on a socially accepted value as unassailable as the sacredness of motherhood.

Noël Coward, although he was not averse to the occasional commercial exploitation of sentimentality, wrote in one of his more clear-sighted moments: 'Mother love, particularly in America, is a highly respected and much-publicised emotion, and when exacerbated by gin and bourbon it can become extremely formidable.' (From *Future Indefinite*.)

The social value of this exaltation by our civilisation of the supreme virtue of motherhood – at almost any cost – has come under scrutiny in the light of the controversy which surrounds the questions of parental surrogacy and in-vitro fertilisation.

In the era of the women's movement it is demonstrably no longer true that childlessness is regarded, as it once was, by a majority of women as almost a badge of shame with a concomitant psychological scar of 'unfulfilment'. More and more women who are fertile choose not to have children and feel no compulsion to apologise for their decision.

But there are still women with some reproductive deficiency who are prepared to go to almost any lengths and expense to become mothers by the grace of modern medical technology.

I suggest that on a gravely overpopulated planet – whose resources are stretched to the limit to feed the excessive number of mouths crying for nutriment, and where growing numbers of the young are homeless and unwanted – it is high time to discard the halo of motherhood and to have a close look at the use of public resources for the promotion of artificial fertilisation. It is time to reverse the social and moral pressure on people to have children. In today's world, fewer is better.

Last week, the NSW Law Reform Commission recommended prosecution of anyone who knowingly arranges surrogacy – where a woman acts as an incubator to carry a baby to term for a couple, either through IVF fertilisation or natural insemination – or assists in such a birth.

There was an immediate reaction from medical experts involved in IVF technologies, warning that if such legislation went ahead, it would merely drive underground or interstate or overseas the irrepressible demand of infertile couples to have children.

For some reason I was reminded of the high-minded protestations of the legal profession whenever a suggestion is made for an alteration of the law (such as their monopoly on conveyancing) which would diminish their opportunity for enrichment.

There is no shortage of sob-stories to feed the motherhood hunger which has long been touted as a natural, applaudable human instinct.

On the day the Law Reform Commission's recommendation was reported, a married couple were pictured standing alongside the cot of their eighteen-month-old daughter, lamenting the threat which that recommendation posed to their desire for another child, a companion to the first. They cannot have another by the normal process of procreation because the wife has undergone a hysterectomy.

A recent story in a Melbourne paper told the tale of a forty-year-old woman who 'knows all about the pain and joys of embryo-making the IVF way'. After getting on to the IVF program at a Melbourne hospital she had several 'goes' (or egg pick-ups), one miscarriage, two major operations to her reproductive system and a labour which left her ill. Finally she bore a child but concluded: 'I'm not willing to go through that again.' Surprise, surprise!

Last year, the Australian Family Association, which has an Australia-wide membership of 5000, recommended to the Federal Government that no more Government money should be used to prop up IVF programs and recommended an end to all Medicare rebates for IVF. The association estimated that the Government bore 56 per cent of the total cost of individual treatments on IVF programs.

In 1987, IVF was estimated to have cost $30 million, of which the Government paid $17 million. That may seem like chickenfeed in today's fiscal figures but as the association's secretary pointed out: 'There's nothing to say it won't be $70 million in a few years time. We're looking at potentials for a huge blowout.'

It has been estimated that the average cost to the health system of a baby through an IVF program (at July 1988 prices) was $42 927 – forty-five times more than the cost of a child born naturally.

The chances of successful IVF treatment are still small. Only 6.9 per cent of IVF treatment cycles actually produce a live-born baby. Children from IVF programs are much more likely to need special care and additional hospital treatment than naturally born babies.

Surely it is time to ask whether the already overstrained health-care resources can continue to pander to this overcosseted hunger for motherhood.

I can already hear protests that it is presumptuous for a man to pass judgment on a subject that is peculiarly within the province of woman's sensibilities.

But I believe countervailing considerations outweigh the rights of couples with impaired procreative capacity to have gratified their desire for a child. Quite apart from the inevitable legal and emotional problems to which surrogacy must give rise, the disproportionate cost of the use of precious medical skills in the IVF program is, in my view, socially unwarranted. Not to mention the basic indignity of using a woman's body purely as an incubator.

A positive use can be found for the frustrations involved in being deprived of the power to have a child. On the same day that the Law Reform Commission's recommendations were announced I read of a scheme under which women volunteer to give one day a week to providing companionship for disadvantaged and unwanted children. Why not try the therapy of giving rather than demanding?

9 March 1989

PUTTING SEXIST ATTITUDES THROUGH THE WASH CYCLE

A few weeks ago, there appeared in the 'Relations' column of the *Sydney Morning Herald* a piece by a man whose marriage had ended after nineteen years, and who was suddenly confronted with the task of being housewife to himself and his twin sixteen-year-old sons.

'In terms of housework,' he wrote, 'I'd always considered myself a "good husband".

'I had changed nappies and bathed babies; I ironed, I washed-up.

'Sometimes I'd bring in the washing.

'Every so often, I'd cook.'

But he soon discovered that such chores are only the tip of the iceberg and that there's much more than that to keeping the show on the road.

Almost every woman I know enthused over this piece. Here was a *man* admitting that he had sponged on his wife's energy and effort throughout his married life!

I don't know how many of my male friends read the piece, but certainly none of them remarked on it to me.

But recently, a similar experience has befallen me.

Not that my wife has left me, but she set off a couple of weeks ago on a six-weeks holiday in South America, the Galapagos Islands and New York.

For a couple of weeks before she left, she became increasingly clucky about whether I was equipped to survive her absence.

I too have, at least for the past twenty years or so, considered myself a reasonably enlightened husband who has shed the worst habits of male chauvinist piggery and pulled his weight with the household chores.

But my wife understood that I didn't know the half of it. She left me a typed list of what perhaps Barrie Unsworth would call the 'basics'.

I had often hung out the washing, so I knew that after the cycle finished, I had to push the knob in and wait for a couple of minutes before opening the door to extract the clothes.

But ensuring that the washing actually happened had never been my province, so I had to be told (in printed form so that I would gradually master the habit) how to *start* the washing machine.

I have always put the garbage tins out, but I had to be reminded that the various small wastepaper baskets in the bathrooms, bedrooms, living room and study had to be emptied before garbo night.

I have frequently fed the cat, but where does her food come from?

I had to be shown that, and also be taken to the supermarket to have pointed out to me where they store the toilet paper and the detergents, etc.

I have now been reminded by experience that these are not one-off, but recurring, tasks. If you forget to keep up the supplies, you are in trouble.

When I told a woman friend about the humiliating detail of my wife's survival instructions, and suggested mildly that I was being treated like a child, she riposted: 'No, like a man.'

Despite the many achievements of the feminist movement in changing men's traditional attitudes, it is still as difficult for even the most enlightened man to shed all of his sexist attitudes – of which he may not even be conscious – as for the proverbial camel to pass through the eye of a needle.

The enlightened man (and I use that expression conscious of its limitations) is shamed by the coarsely sexist remark which is still par for the course almost everywhere where men foregather.

But how many of us have the courage on such occasions to tell the offender, who had naturally assumed we would share his prejudices, that we find his remark offensive or merely put him down with a well-directed barb?

In not doing so, we make ourselves accomplices in his sexism.

A short time ago, at dusk, I left home to go on a small errand.

The area where I had to walk is rather poorly lit and as I crossed to the other side of the street, I became conscious of a woman walking in the same direction ahead of me.

I wanted to pass her and quickened my stride.

As I got nearer to her, I noticed her gazing nervously over her shoulder, so I called out: 'Don't worry, I'm a harmless geriatric.'

She was reassured and I accompanied her to where the light got better and there were other people about.

When we parted, it occurred to me, belatedly, that my conduct had been insensitive in causing her apprehension in the first place. I could easily have walked on the other side of the street.

But men are often oblivious of the fear which, in a world of man-made violence, must be aroused in the mind of a woman walking alone by the sound of overtaking male footsteps.

In short, I am confessing to my discovery of what I saw described recently by a feminist writer, of traces of my own 'unreconstructed masculinity'.

I had thought myself liberated, but I can see that I will never completely make it. In extenuation, I suggest that it is barely possible for a man of my generation to 'reason his way out of' male chauvinism.

I have tried and will keep trying.

Like charity, sexual discrimination begins at home.

I imbibed with my mother's milk the notion of the roles of men and women in society, which is the foundation stone of sexism.

There were already feminists around in those days, notably the Pankhursts, mother and daughter, but their writ did not run very far.

A couple more generations were to come and go before the great feminist teachers such as Simone de Beauvoir, Gloria Steinem and Germaine Greer were to make a slight dent in the male carapace.

But the liberation of men from their sexist hang-ups has been an arduous, and has sometimes seemed to be an impossible, task.

The big hope is that the liberated mothers of today will help to break the mould by convincing their Little Waynes that the possession of a penis does not confer the right to treat women as second-class citizens.

While writing this, I have been painfully conscious that there is nothing original in what I'm saying. But I hope the fact that it comes from a man may help the cause a little.

23 September 1987

IN PRAISE
OF THAT WARM INNER GLOW

Our neighbours in the mountains are, like us, fugitives from the diminishing delights of city life. Though they have been there for only two years and are, by conditioning and temperament, about as urban as you can imagine, they have become moun-tainised with remarkable rapidity. This is nowhere better exemplified than in their neighbourliness.

The Bride and I have so far maintained tenuous ties with the Big Smoke and when we have been absent for a few days, we have always known, even without asking, that the slightest sign of a wilting plant will propel one of the neighbours on to the end of a hose in our garden, while our Otto is never left out on the edge of the road as a challenge to the odd loutish driver of a battered Falcon.

For those unfortunate townies who don't enjoy this wonderful service, an Otto is a large municipally supplied rubbish bin on wheels which we are required to leave on garbage-collection day with one particular side facing the edge of the road surface.

An iron arm attached to the garbage truck grabs it, empties it, and places it back on the edge of the road.

If you don't collect it and put it back within the boundaries of your property, it can be a nuisance to passing motorists.

In short, our neighbours have more than earned the right to a little reciprocal solicitude from us.

You have to understand this pervasive feeling of neighbourly obligation which is a feature of life in the mountains to understand the anecdote which follows.

We recently arrived at our rural retreat late one afternoon, knowing that our neighbours would have left shortly before and would be absent for a few days on a visit to relatives in Taree.

On the way from the car to our front door, The Bride's eagle eye was caught by a flashing bluish-white light in our neighbour's kitchen, which suggested to her a short-circuiting electrical appliance.

Unlike me, she is quick to envisage the worst possible scenario.

There immediately flashed before her a picture of our neighbours returning a few days later to contemplate a smouldering ruin.

She did not think it worthwhile discussing such a serious practical matter with me, but went straight to the phone and rang our electricity supplier, the Prospect County Council, for advice.

The situation was treated very seriously by the officer on duty, who advised that the power be immediately disconnected.

So she went to our neighbours' fuse-box and did as she had been advised.

But her sense of neighbourly duty was far from exhausted. She knew that she may have saved the house from a conflagration, but what of the contents of their freezer and refrigerator?

Though she felt morally justified in the action she had taken, she did not care to contemplate the look on the neighbours' faces when they opened the fridge in a few days time – in fact, when they opened the front door or even got a whiff from the gate.

She knew that the name of the relatives with whom they would be staying was, well, for anonymity's sake, Jones.

She rang telephone information and got the numbers of all the Joneses in Taree and rang all six or seven of them. She drew a blank in each case. (It transpired that the relatives did not live within the boundaries of Taree, but in an adjoining town with a separate telephone listing of its own.)

Talk about Frank Costigan or Tony Fitzgerald pursuing baddies down the money trail! She then proceeded to ring every person whom she knew to be among the neighbours' friends both in the mountains and in the Sydney suburb from which they had emigrated, in case they knew where the neighbours could be contacted.

All this, you will recall, was not to save their house, but the contents of their fridge!

Finally, she struck pay dirt. Our neighbours got in touch. There was an innocent explanation of the flashing light. The Bride reconnected the power. The contents of the fridge were undamaged.

The lesson, of course, was that we should have had a key to their house, as we now do.

I am sure there are many such stories from the centres where neighbourliness still flourishes.

I don't suggest that it has disappeared from the big cities, but I suspect that its native element is the small community which can, of course, exist in small pockets of a big city.

If you ride on a New York bus or the subway, you are struck by the apparent impersonality of relationships in a big city. The occupants sit or stand impassively, mostly avoiding eye contact, occupying their separate, private worlds.

They have so honed their techniques of exclusion that even

when some poor crazy boards the bus or train and starts ranting, the passengers don't seem to notice his or her presence.

But you would find that almost all of them, when off the bus or train, have a 'neighbourhood'.

It would not be described as a suburb in the Australian sense, rather a small region where they regularly do their shopping or go to their favourite bar or stroll their dogs in the pocket-handkerchief parks and rub shoulders with their neighbours – in short, their oasis of community in a desert of loneliness. And they refer to this area as their neighbourhood.

The present housing crisis in Sydney has raised for debate, as never before, the question of the best place to live. Most people don't have a large range of choice.

A big section of the population of the mountains fled there from Sydney because of the enormous difference in the price of housing. Inevitably, that gap is now being narrowed.

But it is more than just a matter of housing; for all of its surviving glories, planlessness, greed and corruption are making Sydney a less and less pleasant place to live.

I once had a dear friend who used to say: 'When I grow old, I want to live on top of the GPO.' What she meant was that the older you get, the more you become dependent on the pleasures, the variety of diversions, and the choice of company which are to be had if you live close to the centre of a big city.

She died before she got old, but I sometimes wonder whether, if she had lived, she would have persisted in her resolve.

16 February 1989

THERE IS MORE TO LIFE THAN SIN, UGLINESS AND TRIUMPHANT VILLAINY

I have been taken to task by an eloquent correspondent for fiddling while Australia burns. Since I have been writing this column he has written to me a few times, usually at considerable length.

The basis of his charge is a column I wrote a couple of weeks ago in praise of the relative peace and civility of life in the Blue Mountains. 'Recently,' writes Norm, my chastiser, 'you write like a man who has withdrawn.'

He then proceeds to list the pollutants of life in this country: 'The most wretched collection of grubs holds all positions of political power . . . the pursuit of wealth and pleasure has been held as the highest virtue . . . Australian capitalism at its zenith has created a new species of hoon . . . this modern city, its roaring canyons of glass and steel architectural abortions . . . a pair of beer barons in control of the national economy . . .'

And so on and so on. Well, Norm, you wouldn't get much dissent from me on many of the counts in your bill of indictment, but hold on a moment. Does that mean that nothing in life is sweet or beautiful and that any praise for any exception from your litany of horrors amounts to treason to the cause of righteous indignation and protest?

Years ago, when I was briefly a practising Marxist, I remarked at a meeting of our tiny sect that I had enjoyed an orchestral concert I had recently attended. The dour leader of this little bunch of zealots put me down with the remark: 'Lenin wiped music.' This was based on one of the sacred texts in which Lenin had remarked that Beethoven's *Appassionata Sonata* provoked a desire to stroke people's heads but at that moment in history the paramount necessity was to crack people's heads.

I agree with you that in many respects we are passing through a dark age in which the values which are at the top of your (and my) list are held in widespread disesteem. Surely, it is part of the battle to reinstate these values, to draw attention to better modes of life than are lived by most of the people who are obliged to live in the modern cities which you abhor and which I find increasingly unappealing?

I don't want to embark on anything so boring as a defence of my record of speaking out on behalf of causes in which I believe or against social ills which I perceive. I would rather consider a much more important question implicit in Norm's strictures: the role of the writer as observer, interpreter and critic of real life.

There is at present raging in Australian literary circles a controversy around the question whether the 'right' sort of writing is being encouraged by the Literature Board, which is part of the Australia Council. One faction in this wrangle asserts that there is a bias in Literature Board grants in favour of 'literary authors', depicted as a small coterie who write for each other rather than for the general public and who tend to congregate around Balmain and Glebe, to the detriment of writers who wish to write about 'the important issues in our society today'.

These are listed by a self-important beggar in the literary bureaucracy as police and political corruption, the destruction of the environment, the power of the media and big business, how the share market is manipulated and so on.

It is impossible to gainsay the importance of such issues and the desirability of their getting an airing both in factual and fictional form. Some of the world's greatest literature (Tolstoy's *War and Peace*, Stendhal's *La Chartreuse de Parme*) amounts to fictionalised accounts of great historical events.

I would hope that the great dramas which must lurk in the events occurring all around us will in due course receive the attention of our best fiction writers. So long as we are burdened with our repressive libel laws that seems to be the only way (with the occasional exception of a Fitzgerald Inquiry) that the villainies of people in high places will ever be brought to light – in fictional form in which we will be able to discern even

147

dimly the real prototypes of the fictional characters. Even here the fate of Amanda Lohrey's *The Reading Group* suggests that the tentacles of those self same laws may be used to strangle some of our best fiction.

But some of the world's greatest literature is remote from 'the important issues of our society'. There is no echo of the Napoleonic Wars – which were raging at the time she wrote – in the 'parlour' novels of Jane Austen. The Dreyfus case and the First World War get only incidental mention in Proust's magnificent evocation of Parisian salons, with its concentration on the goings-on of the parasitic nobility and semi-nobility of the time. And perhaps the greatest of them all, Flaubert's *Madame Bovary*, deals with the follies of a provincial housewife.

It is within the gifts of a genius to be able to distil universal, timeless truths from seemingly banal lives and events which have little to do with 'the important issues in our society'.

Stepping out from the rarefied atmosphere of literature into the more mundane world of journalism, it is still a limiting concept that its concerns should be confined to serious issues, and, especially, the exposure of the evils which undoubtedly exist and which have existed in all societies at all times.

There is also room for fun, trivia, satire – even while Rome may be burning. Writers, either of fiction or journalistic comment, who confine themselves to sermonising will soon find themselves without readers. Anybody who doubts that should conduct a little survey of the size of the audiences to whom our priests and parsons preach.

So I am afraid, Norm, I must decline your invitation to confine myself to the role of a Savanarola. I take on board your warning: 'You, dear Jim, think you have escaped to the mountains. Bad news, buddy. They're coming up there after you.'

I know that for people with a social conscience there is no place to flee from the problems of their era. But I refuse to accept your prescription that life consists of almost nothing but sin, ugliness and triumphant villainy. There's plenty of all those, but that's not all there is.

2 March 1989

THE LONG ARM OF
THE LAW DIALS THE PHONE

In order to tell this tale, I need to go back a few years. It was around 1982, I recollect, that I came home from work to be confronted by the spectacle of a police paddy-wagon outside my back gate.

The street was full of neighbours, whose attention had been caught by some recent commotion centred on my house. Inside the house I found The Bride, who had come home shortly before my arrival, being interrogated by a young male detective who was accompanied by an attractive, blonde female detective.

I was informed that a couple of young junkies had broken into the house. The two thieves had been pinched (or, as I came to learn the correct police jargon, 'two male persons had been apprehended') and were safely locked in the paddy-wagon.

How had this smart piece of police work occurred? Well, the two lads had been a bit unlucky. Dawn Fraser (yes, *the* Dawn Fraser) was a friend of a near neighbour, and we often exchanged pleasantries with her when she was visiting.

Dawn was out walking her friend's dog when she noticed the two male persons behaving suspiciously. She kept an eye on them and saw them go through our back gate. She raced back to her friend's house and called the Waverley police. The officer who answered Dawn's call received the galvanising message: 'It's Dawn Fraser here. Two men have just broken into Judge McClelland's house.'

It would be nice to think that the response which this message evoked is one which can be expected by *all* citizens, whatever their positions in life and no matter how insignificant the messenger may be.

The custodians of the law were on the scene so fast that the poor kids trying to finance a fix were caught red-handed. All they'd had time to purloin was a cheap transistor radio and a watch I had stopped using because The Bride had presented me with a better one.

But, sadly, I have to report that my impression of police efficiency has taken a battering during the subsequent history of this incident, which reached its denouement only a month ago – at least six years after it occurred. There have been times when I have wished that the junkies had never been caught.

In due course, I was summoned to Waverley police station to make a statement. I later heard that one of the accused had pleaded guilty and had got a bond. The other pleaded not guilty and, for some inexplicable reason, was acquitted. I put the incident out of my mind. Then, early last year, I was having a morning cup of coffee in a local cafe when a man approached me and identified himself as the detective who had arrived on the scene and arrested the two culprits. 'By the way, I've still got your watch,' he said. 'I'll drop it around to you next week.'

When, after another month, nothing had happened, I again put the matter out of my mind. I even forgot the detective's name.

But I had reckoned without The Bride, to whom I had mentioned my encounter with the detective. The fate of the watch was clearly on her mind. I suggested we should forget about it but her native doggedness asserted itself. She said: 'I think I'll get in touch with a detective at Waverley whom I met through Neighbourhood Watch.' (I'm sure no pun was intended.)

Now, you would think that a police force which could bring off the spectacular snatch I have reported would be able in a few minutes to locate the detective they were looking for when they were in possession of information about the approximate date of the occurrence, a description of the detective and the fact that he had been accompanied by an attractive, blonde detective. (How many of them would there be who had been attached to Waverley Police?) But you would be wrong.

Over the ensuing months we received at least a dozen phone

calls from police officers from just about every police station in the eastern suburbs.

That would not have mattered so much if they had rung at what I consider a decent hour. These days I am no longer so eager to greet the dawn. (Again, no pun intended.) But it became commonplace for our phone to ring about 6 a.m., and a cheerful voice would announce: 'Good morning, sir. This is Sergeant Fitzomacflaherty. Now, about that watch.'

There would ensue a conversation in which I would have to repeat the approximate date of the occurrence, a description of the detective and his female assistant, etc, etc. A month or so later at perhaps 11 p.m., just after I had fallen asleep, the same or another police officer would ring and ask: 'Could his name have been Russo or something like that?' 'Yes,' I'd say. Anything to get back to sleep.

The Bride was asked by one caller for my full name and date of birth ('So we can run it through the computer,' was the reason offered, though quite what relevance this information may have had to the matter remains unclear).

A month later, again at sparrow fart, there would be that cheerful voice that is obligatory for breakfast radio announcers, and evidently for sleep-disturbing policemen: 'I've found a Detective Russo, sir, but he's got no recollection of the occurrence. Now, tell me, about what size was the person in question? Was he a large man?'

I'd told him before that my man was relatively small for a policeman, but I told him again. 'Well, Russo can't be your man, sir, because he weighs about 16 stone.' (He must have decided that a geriatric like me had never heard of kilos.)

Finally, about a month ago, another cheerful voice announced: 'We think we've got your Omega watch, sir. We discovered it while investigating a robbery at Kings Cross.' The Bride, somewhat tartly at this stage, pointed out that, as evidence in a court case, it was inexplicable that the watch had left the possession of the police.

The watch was finally delivered. It was the right one. By the way, it was a *Cyma*, not an Omega. It doesn't go but I think

151

I'll get it fixed and sell it. Not because of the money, but in case someone else pinches it.

I don't think I could go through that runaround all over again.

5 April 1989

Witches go the way of squibbs, serpents and other fireworks

A story which came through on the wire service last week and was shown to me by my editor, but which none of the media considered important enough to print, has tickled my fancy for significant trivia.

It seems that somebody in New Zealand has been combing through the statute book to uncover and expunge cobwebbed laws no longer considered relevant to the health of their polity.

Like Australia during our colonial period, New Zealand adopted most of the corpus of basic British law. That is not an adverse comment on British law, which was one of our most valuable inheritances. But like all bequeathed wealth, it doesn't necessarily last forever.

So a Bill was introduced into the New Zealand Parliament last week which aims, inter alia, to decriminalise witchcraft down there.

New Zealand has always been a bit more Anglophile than Australia, so it is surprising that it has taken so long to follow Britain down the witchless path, since the crime of witchcraft was abolished there in 1951. (Some malicious people have suggested that, if it had remained on the statute book there, it might have created some sort of impediment to the inexorable Thatcher conquest.)

We followed Britain by abolishing the crime of witchcraft in

1971. Our most famous self-proclaimed witch, the painter Rosaleen Norton, was not charged for riding broomsticks or holding covens but for obscenity under the Summary Offences Act, which was repealed in 1979 but is to be brought to life again by Greiner's blue-nosed Government.

But there was a whiff of witchcraft in the prosecution of Rosaleen, since it was alleged that her paintings were inspired by Satanism. Just as well for her that Fred Nile's lot weren't around in those days or she might have been burnt at the stake.

The New Zealand Bill also abolishes the offence of fighting and quarrelling in churches and churchyards. I don't know about what happens in places like Auckland and Christchurch but I doubt whether doctrinal disputations ever generate enough heat over here to lead to fisticuffs.

There is today in Western countries nothing resembling the violent excitement of the Reformation period. All we get are quaint little quarrels over whether Bishop Lefebvre's insistence that the Papist Liturgy should be conducted in Latin merits excommunication; or the polite little skirmish in the Anglican Church in 1985 as to whether the same fate should befall the Bishop of Durham for suggesting that the Virgin Birth and the Resurrection should not be taken all that literally.

The New Zealand cleansers of the statute book decided also that they could get along without the Act for the most effectual suppression of piracy. Once again I don't know if such an Act survives on the Australian statute book but the only kind of piracy we hear about these days is Warwick Capper being pirated from the Swans by . . . who was it again?

Fireworks are commonly accepted today as being devoid of subversive content. Even in China, the fireworks country par excellence, they continue to receive the blessing of the régime. In Sydney the fireworks display from the Harbour Bridge was arguably the least boring event of 26 January.

But to the good burghers of New Zealand some aspects of the pyrotechnical art were once considered to have special social perils. There is a statute named the Squibbs, Serpents and other Fireworks Act which severely limited the scope of such displays.

Today's New Zealand law reformers have decided that such childish delights no longer constitute a threat to the peace, government and good order of their state and the statute is to be abolished.

Australians are notoriously a mite supercilious about the quaint mores of New Zealanders but I suggest they might well take a more respectful look at the legal housekeeping going on over there.

For example, the Kiwis have decided to retain in their Constitution the quaint archaic prescription that 'the King willeth and commandeth . . . that common right be done to all, as well poor as rich, without respect of persons'.

It would be nice to think that our treasurer will have some regard to that hoary old principle, even though none of our rulers has ever taken it seriously, when framing the taxation scale in next year's Budget.

It has long been accepted that the law is an ass, not only in some of its antiquated and irrelevant customs, but in the vast proliferation of regulations and by-laws made under its statutes.

Some years ago an enterprising and irreverent undergraduate at Sydney University decided to exercise his rights under a university by-law, made under its enabling statute, by turning up to his annual exam on a horse and insisting that, as provided by the by-law, the animal be fed at the expense of the university authorities.

The latter displayed more wit than is commonly forthcoming from such bodies today. They fed the horse generously but sent the bill for the fodder to the student because he was in breach of another by-law for not wearing a sword while riding a horse on university grounds.

Pursuant to the provisions of the Licensing Act there was once a by-law which obliged publicans, in the absence of a government morgue in their district, to provide a room in their inn for a corpse found in the street outside. If that was still the law, an extra wing would have to be built on to hostelries on our major highways.

I don't know if there's any moral to this little parable but the thought that strikes me is this: If only it were as easy to exorcise from human consciousness the subterranean prejudices, such as those which has surfaced during the immigration debate, as it is to ease a few antiquated laws from the statute book.

21 July 1988

OF DRAG AND WIGS

It is a bit hard to understand why NSW attorney-general Terry Sheahan found it necessary to throw a stray punch at the barristers after he had climbed into the ring with the judiciary.

Perhaps it was because almost every judge has been appointed from the Bar and Sheahan was suggesting that they come to the bench tainted with original sin.

Hardly any section of society knows better how to defend itself than the Bar, and the accusation that barristers had acquired a poor reputation in recent years and overcharged for trivial work drew immediate howls of indignation from the men in drag and wigs.

There has been a lot of discussion lately about the restrictive work practices which are supposed to bedevil Australian industry and to diminish its productivity and competitiveness. The campaign against such practices, in the wake of the Robe River drama, gathered such momentum that the Prime Minister found the problem worthy of another of his summits. In the Hawke era, that has become the mark of a serious problem.

But to suggest that the professions, especially medicine and the law, may also spawn unjustified work practices is greeted by the practitioners in those fields as being something akin to an attack on motherhood or the flag.

A few months ago I had to consult a medical specialist. I had seen him before and thought it would only be a matter of phoning him and making an appointment. But no, I had to get a referral from my GP.

Similarly, if you know that some barrister is a taxation expert and you want some advice on tax avoidance you can't just go to the barrister and ask for an opinion. You have to see a solicitor who will then refer you to the barrister – and both will charge you.

If you want a silk to represent you in your court case he will insist on having a junior barrister with him, whose function may vary from genuinely helping his leader to merely carrying his books. But you'll have to pay both.

There has been a lot of talk in recent years about modifying the two-counsel rule but in my years on the bench I never had a QC appear before me without a junior.

The leaders of the Bar are very expensive, some reputedly charging as much as $5000 a day. The contest for control of BHP, in which the principal players were Robert Holmes à Court, John Elliott and the beleaguered old guard of the Melbourne establishment, has been estimated to have cost $5 million in legal fees.

Of course the lawyers involved in that skirmish, both solicitors and barristers, were commercial lawyers who are notoriously the most expensive. It is also a matter of prestige for multi-millionaires to hire a mouthpiece who is known to charge like a wounded bull.

In the heyday of common law actions for negligence, which seem likely to disappear in the near future largely because they involve society in such a huge outlay on legal costs, there was a wonderful rort whereby a barrister could 'earn' two or three (or even more) brief fees on one day.

It was done in this way: the barrister would accept a number of briefs in cases which were set down for hearing on the same day. The settlement rate in such cases is high and haggling over an amount acceptable to both plaintiff and defendant might proceed right up to the steps of the court. The barrister holding the multiple briefs would gamble on all, or all but one (which he could then conduct) being settled without a contest and he (or often two of them, a QC and a junior) would be paid brief fees in all of them. The alleged practice of the Robe River workers of demanding that the management provide smoked salmon for their morning tea break does not strike me as all that much more reprehensible.

But the worst feature of such an arrangement was the pressure which it placed on the barrister to twist a client's arm in order to persuade him or her to settle, sometimes for a figure less than the client would have obtained by holding out for what their action was worth and insisting on the matter going to trial. One of the leading practitioners in the common law field, now deceased, was notorious for enriching himself in this way at his clients' expense.

Barristerial reputation – and hence the capacity to command high fees – is sometimes hard to follow. I have watched some of the high flyers in action who are all show and no substance.

I knew one who used to have a swig of champagne before addressing a jury, and whose performance was as flat as stale beer. But there is at least one in Philip Street at the present time who is worth almost anything he should care to ask. Oddly, he does not ask a great deal.

Most barristers are honest, conscientious and hard-working. But there have been, and no doubt still are, a few dopes among them. One thing they are not is underpaid.

So when Mr Roger Gyles, QC, president of the NSW Bar Association, throws up his hands in horror at the suggestion that some of his fellow barristers do not give value for money, don't bother to reach for the handkerchief. Barristers, for all their wigs and fancy dress, are only people.

7 October 1986

DRESSING DOWN OUR LAWYERS

There is surely no aspect of Australian life in which our cultural derivation is more manifest than in the law. The principles of the British common law were imported holus bolus into our jurisprudence and the quaint language of British law became the common currency of Australian lawyers. That is probably what steered one of our most famous sons, Bob Menzies, who boasted of being British to his bootstraps, into a career in the law.

But probably the most slavish and absurd adoption of British legal archaisms was the unquestioning acceptance of the horse hair wig, the 'stuff' (for juniors) and silk gowns (for seniors), the vest, the wing collar and the bib as the appropriate attire for the 'upper branch' (itself a British expression for the Bar) and the judiciary.

Despite the gradual eclipse of the cultural cringe, so eloquently described in Manning Clark's just-published final volume of his monumental *A History of Australia*, our lawyers are fighting a pathetic rearguard action to remain British, despite the trend in every other area to be unabashedly Australian.

True, the last Australian appeal to the Privy Council was disposed of recently. But there is no discernible move in Australia to abandon robing. The barristers' life is an arduous one but they insist on making it uncomfortable as well. In Britain's climate, robing may be regarded as a bit of a harmless tourist attraction, like the Changing of the Guard. In a Sydney summer, it is just plain masochism.

I don't propose to go on about this, because it is a subject I have already pursued ad nauseam.

When I became Chief Judge of the Land and Environment Court, I wrote into the rules of that court an express provision banning robes for judges and barristers.

But no other court has followed suit and the barristers in drag are still a familiar sight around the purlieus of King, Phillip, Elizabeth and Castlereagh Streets and their equivalents in other Australian cities.

My only reason for bringing the subject up again is to point out that our legal profession is in danger of becoming more British than the British.

A friend in England keeps me up to date on British happenings which he knows will be of interest to me.

Last week, he sent me a clipping from *The Times* of August 10 headed 'Barristers ready to discard their wigs as code is modernised'.

The item reports that Britain's Bar Council recently completed a radical overhaul of the profession's code of conduct which will come up for debate before a special meeting of the British Bar next northern spring.

The proposed new professional rules will no longer stipulate that 'wigs shall be worn at all times' and that barristers must wear dark clothes and gowns. Instead they will be advised that they should 'dress in a manner which is appropriate for appearance in court and which will be unobtrusive and compatible with the wearing of robes'.

In short, they may still robe if they want to but won't be refused an audience if they choose not to.

Obviously a barrister in tan shoes with pink shoelaces and a polka-dot vest (remember that great old song?) or sporting a spiky punk hair-do (with or without robes) would find some difficulty in getting the nod from His Honour to open his case.

But the old dark striped suit and an Andrew Peacock or Bob Hawke blow-wave would ensure him a guernsey.

Of course, there are plenty of 'lady barristers' even in England. Presumably, if the new code is adopted, they could get away with anything but a mini-skirt, stretch jeans, a Dolly Parton T-shirt, a Marilyn Monroe cleavage or a Madonna crucifix.

Under the proposed new code, barristers will be permitted for the first time a limited degree of advertising, by being permitted to have their names entered in a legal directory. If the Bar Council has its way, there will also be other quite drastic changes.

Evidently the Bar Council does not presume to advise the judges to get out of drag too, but one imagines that the anachronistic nature of their fancy dress might gradually dawn on Their Honours if they are constantly confronted by un-uniformed advocates wearing the aspect of mere people, which I well know them to be.

Another item in the same issue of *The Times* suggests to me that legal reporting in Australia is all too circumspect and deferential to the judiciary.

The acerbic but very, very far from radical Bernard Levin, discussing the schemozzle which the Thatcher Government has made of attempting to muzzle Peter Wright, author of *Spycatcher*, refers to the 'three judges of the House of Lords – hereafter known as Wynken, Blynken and Nod – who threatened anyone publishing any of Wright's text with transportation to Australia, heedless of the fact that that was where the trouble was taking place. (Free speech has never been safe in the hands of the judiciary, and a more striking demonstration of their instinctive hostility to it would be hard to imagine.)'

He goes on to refer to the conduct of Mr Justice Caulfield in the Archer case (involving that well-known author of airport novels allegedly attempting to bribe a prostitute, who had claimed to have had congress with him, to take a holiday abroad) 'lurching in his summing-up from one egregious error to another'.

The only journalist in Australia whom I could imagine being game to try that tone is Evan Whitton. Can it be that Australian judges are more jealous of their dignity and immunity from scrutiny than English judges and that, accordingly, the notion has got around among Australian journalists that the risk of being cited for contempt of court is greater here than in Britain?

In any event, what a horse laugh would be justified if the British practitioners of the law and the reporters of their doings should emerge as being less mired in the past than their antipodean equivalents, who justify their conservatism by their reverence for British traditions.

28 August 1987

AN ODE TO A LACONIC MECHANIC

There is something about earth-shattering events, such as the consignment of a State premier to oblivion, which tends to concentrate my mind on the mundane. After all what is an Unsworth or a Hawke under the aspect of eternity?

So please pardon the frivolity which is to follow.

Today's anguish can often become tomorrow's wry anecdote. That is the way the tale I'm about to tell unfolds. Early one morning, The Bride and I set out from our mountain retreat in our recently serviced car. Our destination: Adelaide, where the biennial Festival is an excuse rather than a reason – since none is needed – to refresh the spirit with the manifold delights of that city on a human scale.

In due course, we passed a barely noticeable speck on the map which goes by the name of Illabo.

We passed over a railway crossing and found ourselves driving parallel with the railway line. Without any warning, the car, which had been performing right up to its high reputation, emitted a sinister and alarming noise. There was a sound akin to fracturing metal, accompanied by a clanging noise beneath the car, a jerky motion and almost total absence of braking power.

By now, those readers of some mechanical savvy will have diagnosed the ailment. I, who have some difficulty in figuring out how a tin-opener works, waited for the engine's guts to fall on to the road and for the car to collapse in a heap. The Bride, who has much more nous than me about the range of disabilities which can befall a car, was already contemplating the Worst Possible Scenario.

We alighted to have a look for any immediately obvious explanation of our motor's ailments, such as large chunks of metal scattered over the preceding 100 metres. We had been travelling through drought-stricken territory but at that moment it started to rain heavily, the first rain, we were to be told later, seen in the district for nearly six months. We were forced back into the car to wallow in what looked like the wreckage of our joyous plans.

Fate is a shameless ham actor, inclined to overdo both agony and ecstasy. While we sat in near-lachrymose misery, a train passed us conveying a lot of 100 brand spanking new cars. I did not have the heart to articulate the remark which sprang towards my tongue: 'Any one of those will do, thanks.'

Later, when the car's and our pain had been cured, The Bride was to confess that the same thought had passed through her mind.

The knight in shining armour was not slow in arriving. A car pulled up and its driver unhesitatingly volunteered to interrupt his journey and drive The Bride back to Illabo, where she was able to phone the NRMA in Junee while I minded the car. The courtesy of this country man helped to turn our spirits around a little.

In due course, one of those wonderfully undramatic NRMA mechanics arrived, listened phlegmatically to our tale of woe and lifted the bonnet with that let's-get-on-with-it air of the doctor saying to the child who has been brought to his surgery by an anxious mother: 'Well, put out your tongue and let's have a look at it.'

We were able to limp into Junee shadowed by the NRMA truck. It was still raining and as we rounded a beautifully restored old pub, a duck was standing on the roadway looking upwards at the rain as though to say Whitlamesquely: 'Well, it's about time.'

The car was put up on the hoist and we could do nothing but stand around waiting to discover if we were in for a week in Junee or in Adelaide. (No slur intended on Junee. It is a charming town with an elegant railway station. But it's hardly Adelaide.)

After about half-an-hour, our laconic mechanic, for whom we had by then developed the affection you feel for the lifesaver who is dragging you out of the surf, came towards us holding a small round piece of metal which had shattered. It was a wheel-bearing. 'It looks as though it hasn't been greased in years,' he said with professional disgust. So much for the recent and expensive servicing of our car.

We would have to wait until he hunted around the town for an appropriate replacement for the fractured bearing. It was at this stage that The Bride decided she needed a brandy. We walked in the rain to the dear old pub. The duck was still standing in the street.

After four hours we were back on the road, the car going beautifully as we uttered the usual self-consoling clichés about how it could have been worse and we could both have been dead, etc.

So, at this point in my narrative, let me pause to remind my readers that in the present age of almost total dependence on the expert, the most important person in their lives is not their doctor or their lawyer or their stockbroker but their motor mechanic.

Raise your glasses to your conscientious, efficient motor mechanic in whose hands may lie the decision as to whether you will spend a week in Junee or in Adelaide – or indeed whether you'll spend another minute anywhere.

Adelaide is a place where your angst is soon assuaged. So far it has been largely spared the ravages of today's developmental Visigoths, although one or two dreary glass towers are rearing above the grace of its Georgian and Victorian buildings.

A reasonably fit septuagenarian can walk from one end of the city to the other. The car does not yet own the place and war has not yet been declared on the pedestrian. The street vistas are sweeping and uncluttered and that hectic frenzy which engulfs our other major cities is missing. The ambience is civil.

The Festival events have been amply covered by others. The food and the wine, if you know where to go, would satisfy Leo Schofield's most rigorous standards. All in all, it seemed a long way and a long time from Illabo.

24 March 1988

FOR THE BEST IN PAPERBACKS, LOOK FOR THE 🐧

PENGUIN

The Penguin History of Australia   John Molony

A history for the people which is an enticing and comprehensive blend of social, political, cultural, economic and environmental history. Included are those so often neglected by historians, the 'ordinary' Australians whose class, race, age or gender rendered them 'unimportant'.

Here is the story of the making of a nation, the slow and painful process by which a people have come to identify with each other and with the land they inhabit. It tells of strangers and of the strange land which they encountered, confronted and, ultimately, came to understand and respect.

While John Molony deals with the strength of the British heritage, he is keenly aware of the richness resulting from its blending with other cultures. Although Molony is not blind to the failures and follies which followed the white peopling of Australia, his thoughtful and timely history is an acknowledgement of the considerable achievements of 200 years.

Don't Take Your Love to Town   Ruby Langford

Ruby Langford was born on Bos Ridge mission, Coraki, on the North Coast of NSW in 1934. She was raised in Bonalbo and went to high school in Casino where she finished second form. At age 15 she moved to Sydney and became a qualified clothing machinist. Her first child was born when she was 17. She has a family of nine children and raised them mostly by herself. For many years she lived in tin huts and camped in the bush around Coonabarrabran, working at fencing, burning off, ringbarking and lopping, and pegging kangaroo skins. At other times she lived in the black areas of Sydney and worked in clothing factories. Now 53, she is the grandmother of 18 children and works part-time at the Aboriginal Medical Service in Redfern.

FOR THE BEST IN PAPERBACKS, LOOK FOR THE

PENGUIN

The Immigrants   Wendy Lowenstein and Morag Loh

Many Australians believe immigrants have made their fortunes running milk bars, delicatessens or small businesses. The reality is that most of them did the dirty jobs – jobs as cleaners, labourers, process workers – where the qualification is to be 'unskilled' and the reward is low wages. This is a compelling work that tells the real story of what immigrants to Australia between 1890-1970 found on arrival.

Captain Cook Chased a Chook   June Factor

A fascinating study of the rhymes, games, insults and other folklore that make up the rich world of Australian children's culture. It explores the folklore of specific groups such as Aboriginal, colonial and migrant children; it also raises general questions about the nature of childhood, the way in which adult culture affects children and the future of children's play.